Mobile Platform Security

Synthesis Lectures on Information Security, Privacy, & Trust

Editor
Elisa Bertino, *Purdue University*
Ravi Sandhu, *University of Texas, San Antonio*

The Synthesis Lectures Series on Information Security, Privacy, and Trust publishes 50- to 100-page publications on topics pertaining to all aspects of the theory and practice of Information Security, Privacy, and Trust. The scope largely follows the purview of premier computer security research journals such as ACM Transactions on Information and System Security, IEEE Transactions on Dependable and Secure Computing and Journal of Cryptology, and premier research conferences, such as ACM CCS, ACM SACMAT, ACM AsiaCCS, ACM CODASPY, IEEE Security and Privacy, IEEE Computer Security Foundations, ACSAC, ESORICS, Crypto, EuroCrypt and AsiaCrypt. In addition to the research topics typically covered in such journals and conferences, the series also solicits lectures on legal, policy, social, business, and economic issues addressed to a technical audience of scientists and engineers. Lectures on significant industry developments by leading practitioners are also solicited.

Mobile Platform Security
N. Asokan, Lucas Davi, Alexandra Dmitrienko, Stephan Heuser, Kari Kostiainen, Elena Reshetova, and Ahmad-Reza Sadeghi
2014

Security and Trust in Online Social Networks
Barbara Carminati, Elena Ferrari, and Marco Viviani
2013

Hardware Malware
Christian Krieg, Adrian Dabrowski, Heidelinde Hobel, Katharina Krombholz, and Edgar Weippl
2013

Private Information Retrieval
Xun Yi, Russell Paulet, and Elisa Bertino
2013

Privacy for Location-based Services
Gabriel Ghinita
2013

Enhancing Information Security and Privacy by Combining Biometrics with Cryptography
Sanjay G. Kanade, Dijana Petrovska-Delacrétaz, and Bernadette Dorizzi
2012

Analysis Techniques for Information Security
Anupam Datta, Somesh Jha, Ninghui Li, David Melski, and Thomas Reps
2010

Operating System Security
Trent Jaeger
2008

Mobile Platform Security

N. Asokan, Lucas Davi, Alexandra Dmitrienko, Stephan Heuser, Kari Kostiainen, Elena Reshetova, and Ahmad-Reza Sadeghi

ISBN: 978-3-031-01213-6 paperback
ISBN: 978-3-031-02341-5 ebook

DOI 10.1007/978-3-031-02341-5

A Publication in the Springer series
SYNTHESIS LECTURES ON INFORMATION SECURITY, PRIVACY, & TRUST

Lecture #9
Series Editors: Elisa Bertino, *Purdue University*
             Ravi Sandhu, *University of Texas, San Antonio*
Series ISSN
Synthesis Lectures on Information Security, Privacy, & Trust
Print 1945-9742   Electronic 1945-9750

Mobile Platform Security

N. Asokan
Aalto University and University of Helsinki, Finland

Lucas Davi
Intel Collaborative Research Institute for Secure Computing at TU Darmstadt, Germany

Alexandra Dmitrienko
Fraunhofer Institute for Secure Information Technology, Germany

Stephan Heuser
Intel Collaborative Research Institute for Secure Computing at TU Darmstadt, Germany

Kari Kostiainen
ETH Zurich, Switzerland

Elena Reshetova
Intel Open Source Technology Center, Finland

Ahmad-Reza Sadeghi
TU Darmstadt, Germany

SYNTHESIS LECTURES ON INFORMATION SECURITY, PRIVACY, & TRUST #9

ABSTRACT

Recently, mobile security has garnered considerable interest in both the research community and industry due to the popularity of smartphones. The current smartphone platforms are open systems that allow application development, also for malicious parties. To protect the mobile device, its user, and other mobile ecosystem stakeholders such as network operators, application execution is controlled by a platform security architecture. This book explores how such mobile platform security architectures work. We present a generic model for mobile platform security architectures: the model illustrates commonly used security mechanisms and techniques in mobile devices and allows a systematic comparison of different platforms. We analyze several mobile platforms using the model. In addition, this book explains hardware-security mechanisms typically present in a mobile device. We also discuss enterprise security extensions for mobile platforms and survey recent research in the area of mobile platform security. The objective of this book is to provide a comprehensive overview of the current status of mobile platform security for students, researchers, and practitioners.

KEYWORDS

mobile devices, platform security architectures, operating system security, hardware security

Contents

Preface

Personal mobile devices only started appearing outside the laboratory in the early 1990s. In the span of two decades, they have gone from curiosities used by the technically savvy to a mass-market that is fast reaching saturation. Mobile security research caught the attention of the academic research community only during the last decade, when smartphones and mobile applications and services became widely available. However, mobile security as a discipline dates back to the beginning of the mobile communication era in the early 1990s. Today there exists a large body of literature on mobile security and privacy investigating various threats to the existing smartphone platforms and proposing solutions at different levels of system abstraction (hardware, middleware, OS, and applications).

The work that led to this book began three years ago. All of us (authors of this book) were already engaging in active research in mobile platform security, in academia as well as in industry. This book began as an attempt to put the sudden spurt of academic research in mobile security into context, by explaining how and why mobile platform security became so widely deployed. An early version was presented in keynotes at the ACM CODASPY 2011 and at ESORICS 2012. The very positive feedback we received at both conferences, as well as on many other academic and industry related occasions where we presented the work, convinced us that both the research community and practitioners of mobile security would benefit from an expanded, systematic treatment of mobile platform security. This book is the result.

This book consists of three parts. In the first part (Chapters 2–5), we build up a general model for software platform security. We then use the model to conduct a comparative analysis of several representative mobile platform security architectures. We also use the model to derive hardware security requirements and use them to describe widely deployed hardware security architectures. In the second part (Chapter 6) we focus on security extensions targeted for enterprise scenarios. In the third part (Chapter 7), we survey recent research.

We intend this book to be useful to students, active researchers, and practitioners such as application developers. We hope that this book serves as an introduction to mobile platform security for application developers and students, giving them an understanding of the design rationales behind platform security features with which they might already be familiar. Researchers beginning their research on mobile platform security can use the book to familiarize themselves with the state-of-the-art in practice and research.

We are grateful for the valuable feedback from Sini Ruohomaa, Claudio Marforio, and Nikolaos Karapanos on previous drafts of this book. We thank our reviewers, Bilal Shebaro and Aditi Gupta, for carefully reading the final draft. Their feedback led to several improvements in this version. We thank Prof. Elisa Bertino for inviting us to write the book and Diane Cerra for her gentle reminders to keep us to our schedule.

N. Asokan, Lucas Davi, Alexandra Dmitrienko, Stephan Heuser, Kari Kostiainen, Elena Reshetova, and Ahmad-Reza Sadeghi
December 2013

CHAPTER 1

Introduction

In the recent past, there has been a dramatic increase in the popularity of mobile phones that are today commonly known as *smartphones*. Consequently, there is an increased interest in both the security and privacy research community and the industry in smartphone security. Before delving into the topic of smartphone security and privacy, one should define what exactly constitutes a smartphone. The precise definition is a matter of debate [89], but from the security and privacy point of view some significant characteristics stand out. One is the ability to extend the functionality of the device by incorporating new software components. At the moment, this takes the form of installing new applications. Another is the ability to access, and be accessed from, the Internet. A third is the presence of private or sensitive information, such as personal messages, pictures, and location.

Two important observations can be made from these attributes. First, all the attributes have been present in a large class of mobile phones commonly known as *feature phones* for a long time. For example, the Java ME platform [100] that has been deployed to over three billion phones [112] has enabled third-party developers to write and deploy mobile applications for more than a decade. Personal information, such as address book entries, has been stored in mobile phones since their inception. Such similarities imply that the current smartphone security challenges and requirements are not entirely new, and instead of focusing on current smartphones alone, one should study mobile security more broadly. Second, these attributes are instantly recognizable as characteristics of any personal computer (PC) platform, and it becomes relevant to ask, what are the main differences between mobile and PC platforms in terms of security and privacy.

1.1 MOBILE SECURITY HISTORY

Personal computer platforms started out as open systems with few platform security mechanisms in place. In PC environments, users have been allowed to install new applications freely and modify system functionality to some extent. This openness has led to many security problems, including widespread malware. Even today, security mechanisms in PC platforms are primarily based on perimeter control, like firewalls, and reactive mechanisms like anti-virus tools. Although various platform security architectures, such as Security-Enhanced Linux [90], have been designed and implemented, none has seen widespread deployment. The Trusted Computing initiative [137] has specified *trust anchors* that are currently realized as a hardware security component called the Trusted Platform Module (TPM) [138]. TPM chips have been deployed in many PCs over the last decade, but the adoption of hardware security services and applications has been limited to recent devices and few specific use cases, such as hard drive encryption [15, 143], and more recently secure boot [99].

The evolution of mobile platform security has taken a considerably different path. In contrast to PC platforms, mobile phones began as closed systems with limited functionality. In the first mobile phones, third-party application installation was not possible, and the only connectivity was to trusted cellular networks. The early mobile phones did not require protection against malicious applications or network attacks; instead, the mobile device manufacturers needed to consider *other* types of threats. In many parts of the world, mobile network operators provide subsidized phones to their customers in return to commitment to a specified contract period. They require mobile phones to incorporate mechanisms to enforce applications like subsidy locks, to prevent a customer who received a subsidized mobile phone from switching operators before the end of the subsidized contract.

Other stakeholders have imposed additional security requirements for mobile devices. Regulators, like the Federal Communication Commission in the US [2], are interested in aspects affecting the public good. During manufacture a mobile phone undergoes a configuration process where the parameters for radio frequency (RF) operations, like transmission power, are calibrated and stored. Regulators want to ensure secure storage of RF parameters for end-user safety. Tampering with RF parameters could cause defective device operation with excessive transmission power, and harm the user in the worst case. Besides user safety, secure storage of device parameters is needed to prevent users from abusing shared resources. If a malicious user could manipulate wireless transmission parameters on a mobile device, he could gain unfair advantage in terms of bigger communication bandwidth or disrupt communications for other users. Regulators are also interested in theft-deterrence, such as the means to track stolen devices. Mobile device manufacturers have been required to introduce security mechanisms that implement such regulatory requirements.

Some of these requirements made their way into standards specifications. The European Telecommunications Standards Institute (ETSI) [1], the body that originally specified the GSM standard, had representatives from mobile device manufacturers, mobile network operators, as well as regulators. In the early 1990s, a version of the ETSI recommendation on security aspects described protection of the IMEI (International Mobile Equipment Identifier, a unique code for a specific device) and the IMSI (International Mobile Subscriber Identifier, a unique code for each subscription) by specifying that both IMSI and IMEI require physical protection. Physical protection means that "*manufacturers shall take necessary and sufficient measures to ensure the programming and mechanical security of the IMEI*" [45]. Immutability of IMEI and IMSI is essential for enforcing subsidy lock, as the network operators want to bind a subscription to a specific mobile device. Immutability of IMEI also serves as a theft-deterrent mechanism. In many countries, the law enforcement authorities want to have the ability to track stolen mobile devices. A subsequent version of the same ETSI specification re-iterated the requirement that the IMEI must not be changed after the mobile equipment final production process. "*It shall resist tampering, i.e., manipulation and change, by any means, e.g., physical, electrical and software*" [46]. The specification also implied that compliance to this requirement would be needed for *type approval* (i.e., a permission from regulatory authorities to sell a device in a particular country). To meet these regulatory requirements, mobile device manufacturers needed to introduce security mechanisms for integrity protection of data stored on device, such as device identifiers.

While PC security mechanisms have traditionally addressed *external* threats, mobile phones have required protection against *insider* adversaries that have physical access to the device. In applications like subsidy lock, the owner of the mobile device may have an incentive to circumvent restrictions regarding operator change. Mobile devices are also often lost, lent, and stolen. Purely software-based security mechanisms are not resistant against adversaries with physical access to the device. To prevent simple device tampering, mobile device manufacturers needed to introduce *hardware-based* security mechanisms on their devices.

In the early 2000s, mobile phones started gradually opening up for third-party application development with the introduction of application platforms like Java ME [100]. Unlike in early PC platforms, where malfunctioning system software or malicious applications were usually seen merely as a nuisance to the user, in a mobile phone malicious software can cause considerable harm, for example, by making phone calls that result in monetary loss. Besides protecting security-relevant system resources, such as access to the cellular modem, mobile platforms needed to protect personal user information stored on devices. The early mobile phones contained limited private information, such as address book entries. As more features were integrated and mobile phones gradually developed towards the type of devices that we currently know as smartphones, the amount of private user information on these devices grew dramatically. Modern smartphones store a wide range of personal data including emails, pictures, passwords, browsing history, and location information. Company confidential data is also increasingly stored on smartphones. To retain the reliability and end-user trust of closed mobile phones while moving towards more feature-rich, open mobile platforms, the mobile device manufacturers needed to introduce *platform security architectures* that control the execution of untrusted third-party applications on the device.

To summarize, the evolution of mobile platforms has taken a different path from PC platforms in three significant ways. First, while PCs started as open platforms where few control mechanisms for installed third-party applications were in place, the early mobile phones were closed systems and the opening of these platforms was performed in a more controlled manner by introducing necessary platform security mechanisms. Second, in many mobile use cases the adversary may have physical access to the device, and thus from the very beginning, mobile devices needed to include hardware-security mechanisms that are resistant to simple device tampering and software modifications. And third, the development of mobile security has been influenced by requirements from external stakeholders, most notably network operators and regulators.

1.2   BOOK OVERVIEW

The objective of this book is to provide a comprehensive overview on the current status of mobile platform security, including software-based operating system and application platform security techniques, hardware-based device security mechanisms, and current research topics in mobile platform security. While the primary focus of this book is on smartphones, most of the discussion applies to mobile devices of other *form factors*, such as tablets, that are often based on similar software and hardware architectures.

In this book, we present a generic *model* for mobile software platform security architectures. This model describes commonly used security techniques in mobile operating systems and application platforms, and identifies requirements for hardware security mechanisms in mobile devices. This model serves three purposes. First, it explains how current smartphone security architectures work internally, and thus provides a useful resource for anyone that wishes to learn about smartphone security. Second, the model identifies significant security concepts, components and functionalities in mobile platforms and provides a list of *design decisions* that mobile platform designers have to make. These components and design decisions provide a structure for systematic analysis and comparison of mobile platform security architectures. Third, the model can also serve as a reference for designers of future mobile platforms.

We describe the model in Chapter 2, introduce several noteworthy mobile platforms in Chapter 3, and analyze these platforms in more detail in Chapter 4. This analysis highlights the fact that most of the security mechanisms used in currently popular smartphone platforms are not, in fact, new, but borrowed or adapted from earlier research and commercial systems, and thus our analysis illustrates the historical development of mobile platform security. In Chapter 5, we explain typical hardware security mechanisms that are used in mobile devices today, and discuss how such hardware mechanisms can be implemented in practice. Chapter 6 focuses on enterprise security extensions, and in Chapter 7 we discuss research problems that have attracted considerable attention recently, including privilege-escalation attacks, malicious application detection, and application hardening. For each of these problems we present recent solutions from the research community, and identify topics for further work.

Mobile security has drawn significant interest in the research community and industry in recent years. This increased interest in security mechanisms of mobile devices has resulted in a large number of publications on mobile security, including several recent surveys [18, 39, 41]. While these surveys primarily study mobile security in the context of few currently popular platforms, our goal in this book is to address mobile platform security more generally. We define a model that enables analysis of different types of mobile platforms, and we include both historically significant and emerging platforms to our analysis. Our research survey illustrates the latest developments in mobile platform security. We hope that this book offers useful insights to students, researchers and practitioners alike, and serves as a useful resource to anyone who wants to study mobile platform security, or design security architectures for future mobile platforms.

CHAPTER 2

Platform Security Model

In this chapter, we define a generic *model* for mobile platform security architectures. Our objective is to use the model to explain commonly used security mechanisms and components in mobile devices. Many aspects of the model are present in all currently noteworthy mobile platforms while others are present only in a subset. The model incorporates high level concepts, however the exact implementation details may differ from one platform to another. As part of the model description, we identify *design decisions* that mobile platform designers have to make. These decisions serve as a list of significant platform security features that we use for more detailed comparison in Chapter 4. As a part of the model description, we also identify requirements for hardware security functionality which we discuss further in Chapter 5.

We start this chapter by explaining the different stakeholders that are involved in mobile ecosystems and provide an overview of the model. After that, we explain platform security mechanisms by considering a typical mobile application lifecycle, starting from software development to application installation and runtime protection. Finally, we discuss platform management.

2.1 STAKEHOLDERS

Several stakeholders are involved in a typical mobile device ecosystem. Each of these stakeholders, shown in Figure 2.1, have their own assets to protect and adversarial models to consider. Here, we briefly introduce these stakeholders and explain their respective incentives.

Users. Users are interested in the protection of their personal data, such as messages, contacts, and location information to ensure their privacy. Users also want to prevent device misuse that could incur costs for the user (e.g., unauthorized calls and SMS messages). Users want protection against device loss and theft, for example in the form of ability to locate or lock a lost device. Some users want to utilize the functionality of the mobile device fully, without restrictions imposed by external parties (e.g., install any operating system or use any mobile network).

From the user point of view, the primary adversary is typically an external attacker that attempts to extract personal user information from the device or perform unauthorized operations with the device. For remote adversaries, a common attack is to trick the user into installing a malicious application on the mobile device. More sophisticated remote adversaries may attempt to circumvent mobile device platform security protections via vulnera-

Figure 2.1: Stakeholders in mobile device ecosystems.

bilities that can be exploited over a network connection. Moreover, adversaries that obtain physical access to the device are relevant, as mobile devices are often lost and stolen.

Manufacturers. Device manufacturers must meet regulatory requirements and specifications. Examples of such requirements include protection of mobile device identifiers and hardware configuration parameters. Users should not be able to manipulate device parameters, such as battery charging levels or wireless interface configuration settings, as these modifications could lead to device breakage or even potential harm to the user, and the device manufacturers might be held liable. Device manufacturers may also want to control the version of the operating system that can be run on their devices, because of brand protection and business agreements with the platform provider.

The primary adversary for device manufacturers is a user (i.e., device owner) with physical access to the device. The user can try to modify device parameters for personal benefit or modify the operating system that is run on the device. Such device modifications typically require some knowledge from the user, or at least the user must be able to follow instructions that are often available online. While considering users as adversaries, device manufacturers also want to protect users from external threats. Thus, the remote and physical attacks that apply to users are relevant for device manufacturers as well.

Mobile operators. The primary interest of mobile operators is to protect their business model: when a user is given a subsidized device in return for a contract period commitment, users should not be able to use the device with the subscription from another operator. In some cases, protection of the operator business model may include measures to limit mobile device functionality. Examples include mechanisms to prevent users from installing applications that enable Internet voice calls or wireless network tethering. Some operators also want to prevent users from installing mobile operating system variants besides the operator supported ones, and in some cases the operators want to restrict application installation (and purchase) to their own application marketplaces. Operators' interests also include protection against fraud that would cause monetary losses to the operator, such as device cloning and false service bills.

For operators, the primary adversary is a device owner. The device owner may want to bypass the above-mentioned restrictions by following available online instructions in order to use their devices freely. Operators have to also consider more organized (professional) attackers that attempt to gain large-scale monetary benefit by circumventing these restrictions, and malicious or compromised devices that could disturb the communication of legitimate users in the mobile network.

Service providers and developers. Application developers, and service providers that utilize their applications, are primarily interested in the protection of the data that the application stores on a mobile device. In some applications, data misuse can cause monetary losses to the application developer or the service provider. Applications that store copy-protected content (e.g., music) and credentials of monetary value (e.g., payment credentials) provide examples of cases in which application data should not be copied or modified without the service provider authorization. Developers are also interested in the protection of their application code. Purchased applications should not be copied from one device to another without developer authorization, and source code of applications containing non-public algorithms should not be easily readable and modifiable.

For application developers, the primary adversary is a remote attacker that tries to extract application data stored on the device. Application developers also need protection against device owners that attempt to copy or modify application data or code.

Platform providers. Mobile platforms, consisting of a mobile operating system and associated applications and services, are developed and maintained by platform providers. Platform providers make application development tools available for developers, issue software updates to platform components, and in some cases publish the source code of the platform to allow developers to create modified platform versions. Platform providers are interested in the protection of platform functionality. For example, a platform provider may want to limit application installation to only authorized application marketplaces.

The primary adversary, from the platform provider's point of view, is a malicious application developer that attempts to exploit possible platform code vulnerabilities. Platform providers also need to consider device owners as adversaries as some platform providers want to prevent users from installing modified platform versions on their devices. Modified platform versions could disable protective measures of platform providers, for example, allow application installation from any source. Such mobile device functionality disabling is often called device *jailbreaking*.

Marketplace operators. Mobile applications are distributed via marketplaces (often also called application stores). In many platforms, all applications are distributed via a *centralized* marketplace operator, while other platforms allow *auxiliary* marketplace operators to provide additional distribution channels. Direct application distribution from the developer to the device, without a trusted authority in between, is called application *sideloading*.

The incentive of a marketplace operator is to protect the marketplace content (and brand). Marketplace operators wish to provide as extensive collection of applications as possible, and at the same time prevent distribution of malicious applications through their store. The primary adversary for marketplace providers is a malicious developer who attempts to distribute malware through the marketplace. Marketplace providers also need to consider users who attempt unauthorized copying of paid applications or application content.

Administrators. Many mobile devices are owned by companies and used by their employees for both work purposes and personal activities. The incentive of the company that owns the device is to protect company confidential data (e.g., emails and documents) stored on the device. We call such stakeholders *administrators*. Administrators want to prevent malicious applications from accessing confidential data on the device, and also to prevent unauthorized usage of the mobile device functionality that could result in costs for the company (e.g., calls and SMS).

For corporate administrators, the primary adversary is an external attacker that attempts to extract company confidential information from the device or perform unauthorized operations on the device using malicious applications and platform vulnerabilities. Administrators need to also consider adversaries that gain physical access to a company-owned device, due to a device loss or theft.

Table 2.1 summarizes the incentives of different stakeholders, and the respective resources to protect and adversary models to consider. In many cases the incentives of stakeholders can be contradictory. For example, users (i.e., mobile device owners) want to maximize the available functionality on their devices, while device manufacturers, mobile operators, and platform providers may need to limit the available functionality. Designing a mobile platform security architecture that protects only the assets of only some of the stakeholders would be fairly straightforward. The mobile platform security architectures discussed in this book attempt to find a balance in meeting incentives of *all* involved stakeholders which is considerably more difficult.

2.2 MOBILE SOFTWARE ARCHITECTURE

In this section, we provide a high-level overview of a typical mobile device software architecture, as illustrated in Figure 2.2. In modern mobile platforms, third-party developers are allowed to deploy different types of software components. *Applications* are software components with a user interface. Software functionality needed by many software components may be deployed

Table 2.1: Summary of mobile device stakeholders, their incentives and resources to protect, and adversarial models to consider

	Incentives	Resources to protect	Primary adversary	Additional adversaries
Users	preserve privacy, use device freely	private user data	remote attacker	attacker with temporary physical access
Manufac-turers	business model, regulatory requirements	device identifiers, configuration parameters, platform version	device owner	external attacker
Mobile operators	subscriber contract enforcement	usage of subsidized devices, mobile network resources	device owner	external attackers
Developers	mobile service protection	application data and code	remote attacker	device owner
Platform providers	business model	platform functionality	malicious developer	device owner
Marketplace providers	marketplace popularity	distributed applications	malicious developer	device owner
Administra-tors	company business model	company confidential data	remote attacker	attacker with temporary physical access

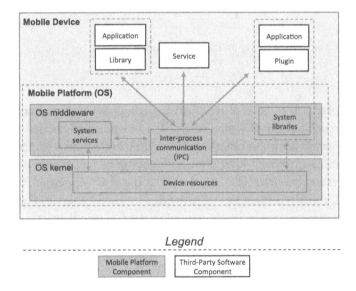

Figure 2.2: High-level model for mobile platform architectures.

as *libraries* that applications and services can link against. *Plugins* extend existing platform and application functionality. (We discuss differences between libraries and plugins in more detail in Section 4.3.) *Services* are processes that can run without a user interface or user interaction. Services can provide APIs for other software components on the same device.

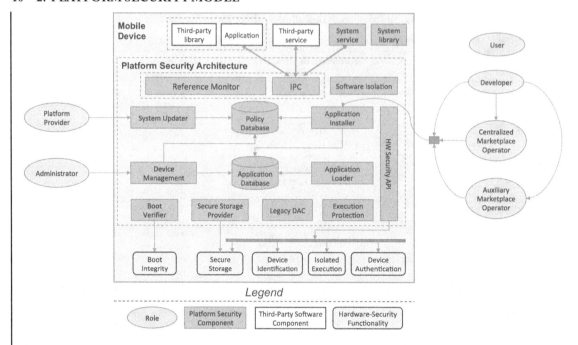

Figure 2.3: Mobile platform security architecture model.

The mobile platform consists of two software components or collections of software components: the *OS kernel* and the *OS middleware*. The OS middleware is a set of system libraries and services that provide common functionality used by both system components internally and third-party applications externally. Communication between applications and services is handled by an *inter-process communication* (IPC) framework. The IPC framework enables an application (or a service) to call functions from an API provided by another service component on the same device. The IPC framework can be implemented in the OS middleware, in the OS kernel, or as a part of both.

Access to mobile *device resources*, such as device peripherals, is typically mediated by the IPC framework and a corresponding system service. For example, to access GPS location information an application makes an IPC call to a system service that provides a location API. This system service determines mobile device location by accessing the GPS peripheral on the device via the OS kernel, i.e., the system service performs a system call to access the requested peripheral. In some platforms, direct access from applications to certain device resources may be allowed. In such platforms, applications perform system calls directly.

2.3   PLATFORM SECURITY MODEL

To protect different stakeholder incentives, mobile device manufacturers and platform providers have developed *platform security architectures* that extend the above highlighted mobile software architecture with security components and mechanisms. Figure 2.3 illustrates a *model* for such platform security architectures. The model contains the involved stakeholders, third-party software components, platform security components, and needed hardware-security functionalities. We explain these concepts in detail in the subsequent sections of this chapter.

The platform security model is based on three basic principles. First, the platform must provide *software isolation* between applications and services. Each applications should be confined to its own execution and storage environment (often called *sandbox*). Applications should not be able to modify execution or access data storage of another application or service, except through well-defined and access controlled IPC communication interfaces. For corporate use cases, the mobile device may need to be divided into separate application *domains*. One domain may be reserved for business applications and company confidential data while another domain is used for non-work related applications installed by the user. We discuss such software isolation mechanisms further in Chapter 6.

Second, mobile platforms support an access control model in which IPC calls from applications to services, and thus ultimately to system resources, are controlled with *permissions*. The platform provider defines access control policies for APIs exposed by the system services, and third-party developers define access control policies for their service APIs. Access to a service API invocation is permitted only if the IPC caller has been assigned the required permissions. Also, other forms of access control checks may be performed, as we discuss later in this chapter.

Third, installed applications are cryptographically signed. Application signing forms the basis for permissions assignment at the time of application installation. For example, permissions that can be assigned to the application depend on the authority that signed the application.

2.3.1   SOFTWARE DEPLOYMENT

In this section we list the main concepts of the platform security model regarding software development and deployment. These concepts form a list of significant design decisions that platform security architecture designers must address. We introduce software deployment related roles and platform security components of Figure 2.3.

Distribution model. The mobile platform may restrict application installation to a single *centralized marketplace* or allow installation from multiple *auxiliary marketplaces*. Applications are installed to the mobile device through an *application installer* platform security component. The mobile platform may also allow direct application installation from the developer to the device (sideloading).

Application signing. Applications must be signed before installation. In platforms with a centralized application distribution model, the marketplace provider typically acts as the centralized trusted authority. The marketplace operator examines the application and signs it, assuming that the application conforms to a predefined publication criteria. The application marketplace operator can also authenticate developers, and issue developer identities that are included in the distributed application installation packages. Developer authentication can use external authentication infrastructures (e.g., a small credit card payment can serve as the developer identity verification). Alternatively, developers can be identified using a developer-chosen key that is controlled by the developer.

The mobile platform may also allow application signing by auxiliary marketplace providers or by the developer. Auxiliary marketplaces can be run by trusted authorities (e.g., network operators) or by third parties. Security guarantees of auxiliary marketplace signing depend on the trustworthiness of the marketplace operator. Developer signing does not guarantee that the application would meet any publication criteria, instead the primary purpose of developer signing is to prove the origin of the application for subsequent application updates. This principle is called *same-origin policy*. Developer signing is needed if application sideloading is permitted.

Application identification. In mobile platforms that use centralized application signing, the signing authority may issue globally *unique* application identifiers to each distributed application. If the mobile platform allows auxiliary marketplaces, the marketplace operator issued identifiers are specific to that marketplace (i.e., each auxiliary marketplace maintains its own identifier namespace). The combination of a marketplace signing key and a marketplace-issued application identifier provides unique application identification.

For platforms that allow application sideloading, the application identifiers must be picked by the developer. The combination of a developer signing key and a developer-issued application identifier provides a unique application identifier. At the time of application installation, a separate runtime identifier that is locally unique on the device may be assigned to the application.

Permission request. At the time of application or third-party service deployment, the developer defines the permissions that the application or the service needs to access APIs that are protected with permissions. Developers request permissions in a configuration file that they include in the application or service distribution package. This file is often called *manifest*. The application installer assigns the requested permissions to the application during installation. In addition to applications and services, permissions may be requested for libraries. If this is the case, the permission set of an application at runtime must be resolved from the permissions assigned to the application and from the permissions assigned to the library that is linked to the application (we explain this in Section 2.3.3).

Access control declaration. The mobile platform provider defines the permissions that are needed to use each system service API call. In a similar manner developers of third-party service components declare access control policies by defining permissions needed for each API call exposed by the service component. This access control declaration is done using a manifest file of the service component. In addition to permissions, access control policies may be declared in terms of application identifiers and vendor identifiers. For example, a service component API call may be allowed only if the caller application originates from a trusted developer.

Access control scope. Besides service APIs exposed through IPC calls, developers of service components (and applications) may be enabled to declare access control policies for other types of resources that the software component controls. For example, the developer of a third-party service could declare access control policies for data files that the service component creates. An example policy could be that only applications with a certain permission can read data files created by the service component.

Access control granularity. The number of used permissions defines the granularity of the access control scheme used. Having a large number of permissions allows *fine-grained* access control policies. For example, separate permissions could be defined for each individual system API call. Such detailed permissions may be difficult to understand both for the developers and for the users. Access control systems with fewer permissions are simpler, but results in *coarse-grained* access control policies that can violate the principle of *least privilege*. If the system supports only a small number of permissions, assigning one coarse-grained permission gives the application access to several, possibly unrelated, system resources that are protected by the same permission.

In platforms where large number of permissions are used, the permissions can be categorized. Permission categorization can be based on the sensitivity of the resources to which they allow access. Another reason for categorization is to enable simplified permission presentation towards developers and users.

2.3.2   APPLICATION INSTALLATION

Next we list platform security model concepts related to application installation and updates. Again, these concepts give us a list of design decisions that platform security architecture designers must address. We introduce application installation-related platform security components shown in Figure 2.3.

Permission assignment. When an application is installed, an *application installer* platform security component verifies the signature on the application and the requested permissions from the manifest file. The application installer consults a *policy database* regarding the requested permissions and the signature. The policy database contains trust roots for signing authorities (typically, public keys of signing authorities) and a list of permissions each authority is allowed to grant. For example, applications signed by the official application marketplace operated by the platform provider may be allowed all requested permissions, while applications signed by a third-party application marketplace could be assigned only a subset of all possible permissions.

Permission assignment may be solely based on application signing by trusted authorities or the installer may ask the user to authorize some of the requested permissions. User involvement at the time of software installation is mandatory when developer signing is used, and user approval may be used to complement authority application signing. For example, access to system resources concerning user data, such as the address book, may be granted based on user approval, while access to more critical system resources, such as the cellular modem, may require application signing by a trusted authority.

Once the application installation package has been verified by the installer component, and the needed permissions have been accepted by the user, the installer assigns the requested permissions to the application and saves the application executables, the set of assigned permissions, and the application identifier to an *application database*. Typically, the application database resides in the device internal memory, although application installation on removable memory elements may be supported as well.

Permission presentation. If a large number of permissions is used, the user may be prompted with coarse-grained permission group labels instead of individual permission names. For example, all permissions that provide access to different type of user data (address book content, emails, pictures etc.) could be grouped together, and when approval for any of these permissions is requested from the user, the same permission group name is presented to the user.

Application updates. Application updates are handled via the application installer. The installer checks that the application distribution package is allowed to update the application components specified in the manifest file. If centralized application signing is used, an application signature by the centralized authority can provide authorization for application update. In platforms that allow application signing by auxiliary marketplace operators, the installer must verify that the marketplace operator that signed the new application version is authorized to update software components distributed by the operator that signed the previously installed application version. We discuss such application updates in more detail in Section 4.2.3.

If the platform allows developer signing, the application installer must verify that the updated application version originates from the same developer, i.e., the updated application version is signed with the same key as the previously installed application version was (same-origin policy).

2.3.3   RUNTIME PROTECTION

In this section we list platform security model concepts related to application runtime protection and introduce related platform security components shown in Figure 2.3.

Runtime permissions. When an application or a service component is started, the *application loader* reads the application permissions and identifiers from the permission database and associates this information to the started process. The loader also links libraries to the created process. If separate permissions are assigned to libraries during installation, the loader determines the application (or the service) process permissions based on the application permissions and the library permissions, or denies library linking if the library does not possess the needed permissions. Once the application process is loaded, the set of permissions typically remains constant. The mobile platform may allow applications and services to voluntarily drop permissions, or gain more permissions by loading a plugin.

Permission enforcement. At runtime, application function calls to system service APIs and third-party service APIs are processed by a *reference monitor* security component. The reference monitor is typically attached to the IPC framework of the mobile platform. Some mobile platforms may support multiple reference monitors. For example, one reference monitor can be implemented in the IPC framework and another in the OS kernel. Such an approach is needed when third-party applications are allowed to make direct system calls (i.e., access device resources of the OS kernel without making IPC calls to system services that mediate access to these resources).

The reference monitor determines caller application permissions and identifiers (e.g., by consulting the application database) and either permits or denies the function call depending on the access control policy of the accessed resource. The reference monitor may also present a *runtime prompt* to ask the user to grant or deny the permission that is needed to access the protected IPC call at runtime. To enable access control enforcement by the IPC call target (callee), the reference monitor can augment IPC calls with permissions and application and vendor identifiers.

Besides permission-based mandatory access control, mobile platforms may utilize existing discretionary access control (*legacy DAC*) schemes. For example, Linux-based mobile platforms can utilize Linux user IDs and group IDs in addition to permissions for controlling third-party software access to system and application resources.

Execution protection. Mobile platforms support various mechanisms for runtime *software isolation* and *execution protection*. Memory areas of different processes must be separated from one another, the process address spaces may be randomized, and dedicated memory areas may be declared non-executable to complicate typical runtime attacks, such as buffer overflow attacks. The purpose of such process execution protection mechanisms is to prevent a malicious application from modifying its code or control flow and affecting execution of other processes. We discuss execution protection techniques in Section 4.3.3, and software isolation in the context of enterprise systems in Chapter 6.

Application data protection. Mobile applications need protection of persistently stored data. A *secure storage provider* platform component enables isolated persistent storage areas for each application. Secure storage functionality consists of two components: data *integrity* protection and data *confidentiality* protection (integrity protection can include data *freshness*, i.e., replay protection). Software-based data protection mechanisms are typically vulnerable to adversaries that have physical access to the device. Security-critical applications, like credit card implementations and payment applications, require protection against simple physical attacks. The secure storage component may utilize hardware-assisted *secure storage* functionality, for data integrity or confidentiality or both. Besides local protection, application data need to be protected when backed up to unsafe, external media.

Hardware security APIs. Software-based isolation mechanisms are vulnerable to implementation errors in platform code. As mobile platforms grow in size and complexity, runtime software vulnerabilities in mobile platform become a relevant threat. Today, software vulnerabilities are found in all major smartphone platforms [48, 148].

Security-critical applications may require hardware-assisted *isolated execution*, i.e., application execution that is not only isolated from other mobile applications but also from the mobile platform. The majority of the current mobile devices support hardware security architectures, like ARM TrustZone [12, 13], that allow small pieces of security-sensitive code to be executed in isolation from the mobile OS. If such a security mechanism is supported by the device, a *hardware security API* component may provide an interface for loading security critical code for isolated execution. Similar hardware security mechanisms that may be exposed to applications include *device identification* and *device authentication*. We discuss these hardware security mechanisms further in Chapter 5.

2.3.4 PLATFORM MANAGEMENT

In this section we list platform integrity and device management concepts of the platform security model. We introduce related platform security components of Figure 2.3.

Platform boot integrity. The integrity of the platform security components introduced above needs to be protected. Platform security components are stored on a persistent storage medium that may be updated through externally accessible interfaces, such as a USB port. If an adversary is able to modify any of these components, he can circumvent the permission-based access control model or any other security enforcements. For example, if an adversary manages to modify the functionality of the application installer component, he can install applications with any permissions regardless of the application signature or user approval. Similarly, if the adversary manages to modify the reference monitor component, he can access any service API call without restrictions. Two common approaches for platform boot integrity protection exist.

First, many mobile device manufacturers enforce hardware-assisted *secure boot* [11]. To prevent an adversary from modifying the platform security components on the device, manufacturers can ensure the integrity of all system components during the device startup. A *platform verifier* component checks signatures over other platform security components with respect to a device manufacturer issued reference values and a trust root that is immutable on the device hardware. Secure boot prevents unauthorized platform component modifications offline (when the device is not running), but restricts device use to manufacturer pre-approved operating system images. Secure boot does not protect against runtime modifications of platform security components; execution protection mechanisms introduced in the previous section are designed for this purpose.

Second, other device manufacturers deliberately allow developers to create custom operating system versions, but record measurements of the booted platform components to integrity protected hardware registers. Such operating system startup process is called *authenticated boot*. These measurements can be used for enforcement of security decisions on the mobile device at runtime, and for reporting the device state to an external verifier. In addition, the adversary should not be able to revert the platform software back to a previous state. For example, the adversary should not be able to restore older versions of platform components with security vulnerabilities, once a new and fixed version of the platform components have been updated to the device.

Platform data integrity. Besides platform security component integrity, the security of the permission-based access control model depends on the integrity of *platform data*, such as the policy database and application database. If the adversary manages to modify the contents of these databases, he may assign arbitrary permissions to previously installed applications, or modify the behavior of installed applications. To prevent such modifications, the platform may support hardware-assisted secure storage (integrity protection), with possible replay protection mechanisms. We discuss such hardware-assisted device boot and secure storage mechanisms in more detail in Chapter 5.

Platform updates. Mobile platforms need updates, both in terms of new functionality and fixes to possible bugs and vulnerabilities. Platform providers issue updates to various system components. On the mobile device, a *system updater* component authenticates system updates using trust roots and system update policies on the policy database. If the update is acceptable, the system updater rewrites parts of the operating system image. In some platforms the system updater is part of the application installer implementation.

Device management. Administrators can send device management commands to mobile devices. Such commands are verified by a *device management* component using trust roots in the policy database. The device management commands may, for example, install new applications to the device, remove previously installed applications, or add or remove new trust roots into the policy database and thus control what type of applications the user is allowed to install. Remote administrators may also modify certain system settings, like mandate PIN code protection for their device, or set the minimum acceptable length of device PIN. Such policy changes are stored into the policy database. We discuss mobile device management further in the context of enterprise security extensions in Chapter 6.

CHAPTER 3

Mobile Platforms

In this chapter we describe six mobile platforms and discuss their security architectures with respect to the platform security model introduced in Chapter 2. For our analysis, we have chosen two *historically* significant mobile platforms, Java ME and Symbian, two *currently* popular platforms, Android and iOS, and two other mobile platforms, MeeGo and Windows Phone, that serve as examples of different types of mobile platforms.

This selection does not include all possible mobile platforms. Other platforms that have been widely used in the past, or are currently emerging, include BlackBerry, Tizen, Sailfish OS, WebOS, and Firefox OS. Many security mechanisms in these platforms are based on the previous architectures that we discuss. Application development in BlackBerry devices, before version 10, is done using the Java ME framework. Sailfish OS is based on the Mer project [3] that builds on the MeeGo platform. The Tizen platform adapts some security components of the MSSF framework [83] used in MeeGo. BlackBerry 10 supports repackaged Android applications. WebOS and Firefox OS are examples of mobile platforms that utilize web application development techniques that are also supported in iOS and Windows Phone platforms.

In all of these platforms, third-party application execution is controlled with a permissions-based access control model and applications are signed and isolated from one another. The intention of our platform selection is to give a representative sample of different types of mobile platforms.

This chapter illustrates how each of the selected mobile platforms fits to the generic platform security model. Our intention is not to provide a detailed technical description on each platform, rather, for more information we provide references for the reader. In Chapter 4 we provide a systematic comparison of the selected platforms which illustrates the similarities, and sometimes subtle differences, these platforms have.

3.1 JAVA ME

Java Micro Edition (ME) is a mobile application platform introduced in the late 1990s. It is not a mobile operating system, but an application framework that can be deployed on top of any mobile OS. Java ME was the first widely adopted platform for third-party application development in mobile phones. We focus our discussion on the widely used Java ME version called MIDP 2 [100].

In the Java ME platform, third-party software development is limited to applications, as developers are not allowed to deploy shared libraries or services. All applications are written in the

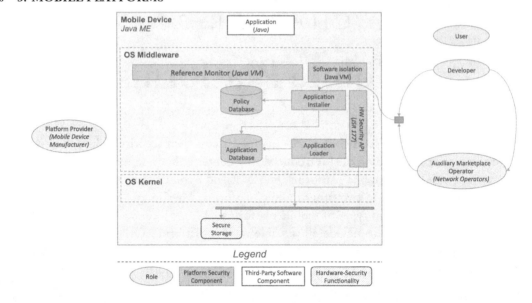

Figure 3.1: Java ME platform security architecture.

Java language. Applications are typically distributed via marketplaces. Application marketplaces are operated by mobile device manufacturers, mobile network operators, and similar authorities. Typically, applications are signed by the marketplace operator. Depending on the requested permissions, an application may not need signing. Application installation policies, stored in the policy database on the mobile platform, define the permissions that application signing authorities are allowed to grant.

In Java ME terminology, each such signing authority-specific policy constitutes a *protection domain*. Typically, Java ME devices have four predefined protection domains: device manufacturer domain, network operator domain, and domains for identified and unidentified third-party applications. Permissions in each policy (protection domain) can be classified into two groups: ones that are allowed by default and those that require user approval at runtime. In addition to application distribution through marketplaces, the Java ME architecture allows application sideloading. Sideloaded applications are usually not signed.

The Java ME security architecture is illustrated in Figure 3.1 with respect to the platform security model described in Chapter 2. Because Java ME is an application framework, and not a complete mobile OS, all platform security components including the application installer and the application loader are implemented as system services and libraries that run on top of the OS kernel. The Java ME platform components can be integrated to any mobile OS.

Application execution is controlled by a Java virtual machine that provides software isolation using typical Java application sandboxing mechanisms and acts as the reference monitor for permission-based access control. Platform integrity verification and updates are not part of the

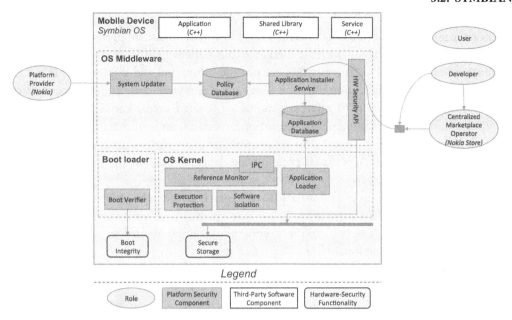

Figure 3.2: Symbian platform security architecture.

Java ME architecture, but the underlying mobile OS may verify platform components and provide authenticated updates. The JSR 177 specification [111] defines an interface through which third-party developers may use secure storage functionality of hardware elements, such as SIM cards.

3.2 SYMBIAN

Symbian was one of the first smartphone operating systems, and the first to include an integrated platform security architecture. The architecture is shown in Figure 3.2 with respect to the platform security model. Symbian supports third-party applications, services, and shared libraries. Development is based on the C++ language. Developers request permissions for each type of software component (application, service, or library). The need for application signing depends on the requested permissions for each component.

Applications and other third-party software components are mainly distributed via a centralized application marketplace (Nokia Store), but applications sideloading, i.e., direct distribution from the developer to the device is allowed as well. Permissions in Symbian architecture are called *capabilities*.[1] Permissions are classified into four groups: User, Restricted, System, and Manufacturer.

---

[1]In many security architectures the term *capability* denotes a communicable token of authority [123]. Despite their name, capabilities in the Symbian platform cannot be transferred from one software component to another.

Symbian is a micro-kernel architecture in which many OS components are implemented as services running on top of the OS kernel [122]. In the Symbian architecture, the inter-process communication (IPC) framework that mediates calls between software components acts as the reference monitor. The IPC framework is part of the OS kernel and it augments IPC calls with caller permissions and application identifiers, so that callees (services) can implement access control enforcement in addition to reference monitor provided access control enforcements [73]. The application loader component and execution protection and software isolation mechanisms are implemented in the OS kernel. The application installer component is a system service with manufacturer permissions. Access to the application database and the policy database is controlled with permissions.

The Symbian platform provides APIs to third-party developers for hardware-assisted secure storage functionality. It also supports hardware-based platform integrity verification. The integrity verification functionality (i.e., boot verifier component) is implemented as part of OS boot loader. Remote management functionality is not part of the Symbian platform, although commercial device management extensions exist.

3.3   ANDROID

Android is a open-source smartphone platform developed by Google. At the time of writing, Android is the most widely used smartphone platform [53]. Mobile device vendors extend the Android Open Source Project (AOSP) described in this section with vendor specific extensions. Android applications consist of the following main components: Services perform non-interactive data processing, Content Providers provide data sharing between applications, Broadcast Receivers receive IPC messages, and Activities are software components with a user interface. Thus, an Android application can function as an "application" or as a "service" using the description outlined in Section 2.2. Android application components interact using IPC calls. Google Play marketplace is the primary distribution channel for Android apps, but application installation from auxiliary marketplaces and sideloading is allowed. Android applications are signed by the developer.

The Android security architecture is illustrated in Figure 3.3. Android is based on a modified Linux kernel with a non-GNU user space environment tailored to mobile devices. Applications are sandboxed based on Linux DAC credentials by assigning each application a separate sandbox which is assigned a separate Linux user ID. Third-party applications cannot run with the root user ID on regular Android versions. Thus, Linux DAC acts as a reference monitor which enforces separation of applications. In each sandbox an instance of a register-based Dalvik virtual machine is executed. These virtual machines execute Dalvik bytecode, which can be created from Java bytecode and is optimized for speed and memory usage. Application development is mainly based on Java. Besides Java applications, third-party developers are allowed to deploy application-specific, native (C/C++) libraries and binaries. Android applications access native library functionality via Java Native Interface (JNI). In a separate, privileged sandbox an instance of the Dalvik VM exe-

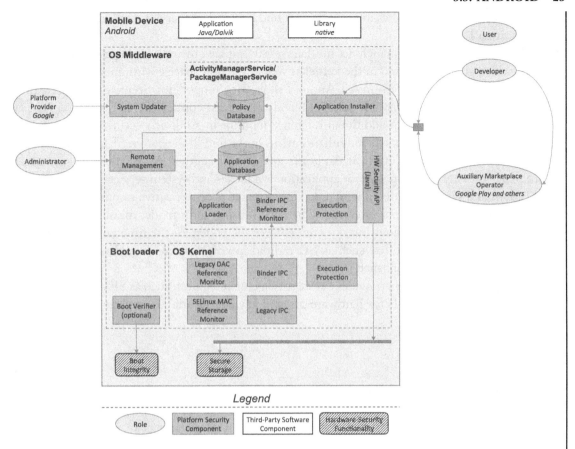

Figure 3.3: Android platform security architecture.

cutes the so-called Android System Server, a middleware component that is part of the platform security architecture. The System Server's sandbox has system privileges and is thus able to access protected device resources in the underlying Linux operating system. Third-party applications trigger most system functionality by issuing IPC calls to components of the System Server and privileged pre-installed system apps which mediate system calls to the OS.

Inter-process communication on Android is mainly based on Binder, a re-implementation of the OpenBinder IPC framework. While the core Binder IPC mechanism is implemented in the Linux kernel, the Activity Manager Service component, in cooperation with the Package Manager Service embedded in the System Server, acts as the primary reference monitor that checks permissions on the Binder IPC. Callees may implement additional access control enforcement. Legacy IPC (e.g., Linux IPC using sockets or pipes) is supported as well. The Activity

Manager Service combined with an additional middleware layer service, furthermore, acts as the Application Loader.

The Android platform includes mechanisms to mitigate memory corruption attacks at runtime, which are implemented in the kernel as well as the user space environment.

In addition, since Version 4.3 Android ships with support for Security Enhanced Linux (SELinux), a Linux Security Module for mandatory access control (MAC) based on type enforcement which acts as an additional reference monitor in Android's security architecture. In combination with SELinux specific enhancements in the middleware layer, SELinux for Android is denoted as SEAndroid [106]. SEAndroid's goal is to strengthen Android's security model by enforcing a least-privilege policy for application sandboxes and system services, thus forcing applications and services to use only intended interfaces to access sensitive resources. On standard Android 4.3 builds, SELinux is currently by default using audit mode, meaning it merely logs access control policy violations but does not enforce the policy. At the time of writing, Android 4.4 with new security features, such as SEAndroid in enforcing mode and new compile-time hardening features, was published [66].

The Android platform provides device management features, such as SELinux audit mode. Android provides also APIs for hardware-assisted key pair creation, encryption, and signatures [63].

3.4   IOS

The iOS platform is used in iPhone, iPad, and iPod devices. In iOS, third-party application development is primarily done in Objective-C, although web applications running on top of the Webkit runtime are also supported. Since Objective-C is a superset of C, it is also possible to write applications in C or C++, or to intermix Objective-C code with C/C++ code. However, it is hardly possible to write an application purely in C/C++, because applications typically need to use Objective-C for the user interface (UI).

Application-specific libraries are allowed, but third-party developers cannot deploy shared libraries or services. Application distribution is limited to a centralized marketplace, the Apple Store, that signs all applications, subject to conformance to Apple application publishing criteria. Application sideloading is not permitted. The iOS platform security architecture is shown in Figure 3.4.

Access control enforcement is based on mandatory access control features of the TrustedBSD kernel [141]. All third-party applications are assigned a single, pre-defined *sandboxing profile* that defines the assigned permissions for all applications [32]. All applications are also assigned the same user identifier. System calls to location information generate runtime user prompts. In recent versions of the iOS platform, the runtime prompts have been extended to application requests on contacts, reminders, calendar entries, microphone and photos [10]. Starting from iOS 6, users can enable or disable access to private information for each application from the system settings.

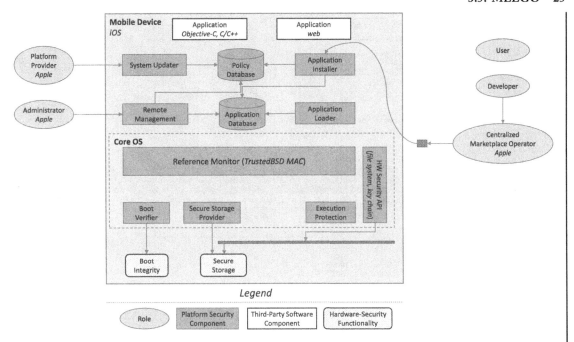

Figure 3.4: iOS platform security architecture.

The TrustedBSD kernel is the reference monitor and enforces access control on application system calls. Fine-grained access control rules are possible using system call arguments. For example, file system access can be controlled based on file names in system calls. Using this mechanism, iOS prevents one application from accessing the persistent storage of another. The platform supports enforcement of code signing; application signatures are verified before application installation and execution.

Built-in platform applications are assigned permissions (called *entitlements*) to perform privileged tasks. For example, the browser is allowed to generate code at runtime. Dedicated system applications are used to access security-sensitive system resources, like messaging, cellular modem and calendar. Recent versions of Mac OS X have added third-party application permissions for system resources like Internet, Bluetooth, and music [8]. The iOS platform version 6 incorporates a similar, more flexible permission model.

The iOS platform supports data and file encryption using a hardware-resident, device-specific secret [9]. Built-in device management features and platform boot integrity verification (secure boot) are supported as well.

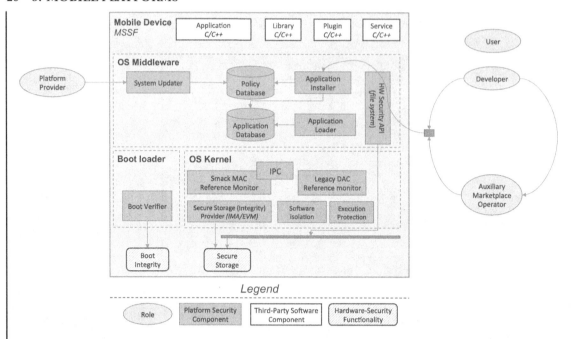

Figure 3.5: MSSF platform security architecture.

3.5   MEEGO

MeeGo was a Linux-based mobile platform that has been used as the basis for the recently introduced Tizen [4] and Sailfish [82] mobile operating systems. The MeeGo platform provided a security architecture called Mobile Simplified Security Framework (MSSF) [56, 83, 96]. In this book, we focus on the MSSF framework. Some security components of MSSF are used in the Tizen platform as well (e.g., Smack access control module described below). The MSSF security architecture is illustrated in Figure 3.5 using the model described earlier.

Application development for MSSF is done in C or C++. Besides applications, MSSF supports third-party shared libraries, services, and plugins. Applications may be installed from multiple marketplaces or directly from the developer (sideloading). Each application installation package is typically signed, although non-signed applications can be installed as well. A pre-installed security policy on the device determines the permissions that each software source, marketplace or developer, is allowed to grant. The policy also defines a numeric *trust level* for each software source. These trust levels are used to control application updates, i.e., previously installed applications may be either updated by the same software source or by software sources with a higher trust level value [139].

Inter-process communication between processes is based on Unix sockets and the D-Bus framework [25]. An access control subsystem acts as a reference monitor for IPC calls. Access to resources on the device is controlled using permissions that are called *resource tokens*, and Linux user IDs and groups. Access control enforcement is implemented using the Smack LSM kernel module [126]. Smack is a mandatory access control system, similar to SELinux used in Android. Whereas SEAndroid is primarily used to isolate applications and system services, Smack handles permission-based access control as well. Besides system APIs, access control can be applied to individual files. Each file and file operation, such as read and write, can be assigned separate permissions.

The application loader is implemented in the OS middleware. Integrity Measurement Architecture (IMA) [121] and Extended Validation Module (EVM) [132] architectures are used to protect device persistent storage integrity from offline modifications with hardware support. However, IMA and EVM do not provide data confidentiality. The application installer authenticates software packages during installation and update. System updates are handled via the application installer. MSSF supports hardware-assisted secure storage that is integrated in the OS file system. Hardware-based encryption does not require usage of specific encryption APIs from the application developer, but instead the file system can encrypt data stored on files. MSSF supports hardware-assisted platform integrity verification. Both secure boot and authenticated boot are supported.

3.6 WINDOWS PHONE

The first versions of the Windows Phone platform utilized the Windows CE kernel. Starting from Windows Phone 8, the OS kernel is shared with the PC Windows version (e.g., Windows 8). Application development is done using C# and the .NET runtime. Windows Phone 8 supports applications implemented using web development techniques (JavaScript and CSS) as well. All applications are installed from a centralized application marketplace that is operated by Microsoft. Third-party development is limited to applications. Background services can be deployed only for pre-defined purposes, such as music playback. Application sideloading is not permitted.

The Windows Phone security architecture is shown in Figure 3.6 with respect to the platform security model. The Windows Phone OS is divided into four protection rings called *chambers* [98]. The most privileged chamber, the Trusted Computing Base (TCB), is used to run the operating system kernel, the device drivers and the application installer. System services are run in the Elevated Rights Chamber (ERC), while pre-installed applications are executed in the Standard Rights Chamber (SRC). Third-party applications installed from the marketplace are run within the Least Privileged Chamber (LPC).[2] Access to protected system APIs is controlled with permissions within the Least Privileged Chamber.

---

[2]The publicly available documentation on Windows Phone platform does not describe the chambers in which platform security components like the application loader and the system updater are implemented. In Figure 3.6, we illustrate them as part of the ERC chamber as this chamber is intended for running system services.

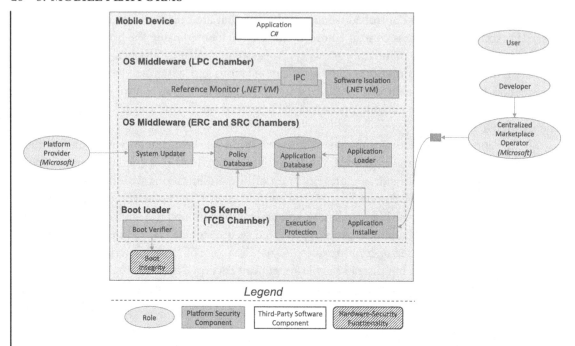

Figure 3.6: Windows Phone platform security architecture.

The .NET runtime acts as the reference monitor. The Windows Phone platform provides built-in support for platform integrity verification (secure boot) and remote management features. No hardware security APIs are provided for third-party developers.

CHAPTER 4

Platform Comparison

In this chapter, we compare the mobile platforms introduced in Chapter 3. We use the main concepts and design decisions identified as part of the platform security model (Chapter 2) as our comparison points. Although all currently significant mobile platforms support a similar platform security architecture, there are many, sometimes subtle, differences. The purpose of this chapter is to illustrate these differences. At the same time, our analysis highlights the similarities among these platforms. Most security mechanisms used in the currently popular mobile devices are not new, but adapted from previous mobile platforms.

Our analysis demonstrates the evolution of mobile security architectures from the early mobile phones to current smartphone platforms. We start with software deployment aspects, and proceed to application installation and runtime protection. Platform management is discussed at the end of this chapter.

4.1 SOFTWARE DEPLOYMENT

In this section we present a comparison of software development security mechanisms. Table 4.1 provides a summary.

4.1.1 DISTRIBUTION MODEL AND APPLICATION SIGNING

Applications are typically distributed via online marketplaces. In some platforms, application sideloading, direct distribution from the developer to the device, is explicitly prevented while in others the ability to sideload applications depends on the permissions requested by the developer.

Symbian applications that require User permissions may be distributed via sideloading, while applications that require permissions from System, Restricted, or Manufacturer categories, must be centrally signed (we explain these permission categories in more detail in Section 4.1.5). Android applications are developer-signed, and thus all third-party applications can be sideloaded. In MSSF, application distribution policies are device manufacturer and network operator specific. Manufacturers and operators may decide to accept distribution via authorized marketplaces only, or to allow auxiliary marketplaces and sideloading. Application distribution in iOS and Windows Phone platforms is limited to a centralized application marketplace that signs all installed applications. On these platforms, application sideloading is explicitly prevented.

Table 4.1: Comparison of software development security mechanisms

	Java ME	Symbian	Android	iOS	MSSF	WP
distribution model	multiple marketplaces, sideloading	centralized marketplace, sideloading	multiple marketplaces, sideloading	centralized marketplace	multiple marketplaces, sideloading	centralized marketplace
application signing	multiple signing authorities	centralized signing and developer signing	developer signing	centralized signing	multiple signing authorities	centralized signing
application identification	package name	application identifier, developer identifier	Linux user ID, package name	application identifier	marketplace, package name, application identifier	application identifier
permission request	applications	applications, services, libraries	applications, services	applications	applications, libraries, services, plugins	applications
access control scope	system APIs	system APIs, application IPC	system APIs, application IPC	system APIs, file access	system APIs, application IPC, file access	system APIs
access control declaration	permissions	permissions, application and vendor identifiers	permissions, Linux AC, application identifiers	pre-defined profile	permissions, Linux AC, application identifiers	permissions
access control granularity	fine-grained, categorized	coarse-grained, categorized	fine-grained, categorized	pre-defined profile	fine-grained	coarse-grained

4.1.2   APPLICATION IDENTIFICATION

Application identifier assignment varies between platforms. Application identifiers in the Android platform are developer chosen package names. The combination of a developer signing key and a package name uniquely identifies an Android application. A locally unique Linux user ID is assigned to each application at installation time by the installer. At runtime, Android applications can be identified either based on the user ID or the application package name. Only applications that are signed with the same developer key can be assigned the same Linux user ID at installation.

MSSF applications can be identified by a unique application identifier that consists of three parts: marketplace identity, package name, and package-specific application identifier. The package name and application identifier are chosen by the developer.

Symbian platform uses a mixed approach. During application distribution the marketplace operator checks that the application conforms to a publication criteria and assigns a globally unique application identifier from a so called *protected range* of application identifiers. The signing authority (i.e., the marketplace operator) maintains a mapping between the issued application identifiers and developer identifiers. If an application does not need permissions that would require centralized signing, the developer is allowed to pick the application identifier from an *unprotected range* of application identifiers.

Windows Phone and iOS platforms are based on centralized application signing. The marketplace operator assigns globally unique identifiers to applications at distribution. Java ME application identifiers are developer-chosen package names.

4.1.3 PERMISSION REQUEST

Two approaches for permission request exist. In Java ME, Android, and Windows Phone platforms, developers request permissions only for application and service components. When an application or a service loads a library, the library inherits the permissions assigned to the application or service automatically.

Symbian and MSSF platforms have adapted a different approach. In Symbian, the developer declares permissions for libraries as well. When an application or a service loads a library, the permissions of the executable process are resolved from the application and library permission sets. In MSSF, the developer can declare plugin permissions that will be added to application that loads the plugin. We explain such application load-time and runtime permission handling in Section 4.3.1.

4.1.4 ACCESS CONTROL DECLARATION AND SCOPE

In Java ME and Windows Phone, access control policies are declared using permissions only. iOS uses a pre-defined access control profile (sandboxing profile) for all third-party applications, and thus all third-party iOS applications have the same permissions by default.

Symbian access control policies can be declared using permissions, application identifiers, and application vendor identifiers. Both application and vendor identifiers are assigned by the application marketplace. The Symbian reference monitor enforces permission-based access control policies declared in manifests, while application and vendor identifier enforcement must be implemented in the service component.

Android utilizes a combination of permissions and Linux discretionary access control. Binder-based IPC between Android applications is controlled with permissions. Linux user IDs and group IDs are used to sandbox applications and to control access to system resources, such as the file system and network sockets. Some permissions for access control on low-level resources, like TCP sockets, Bluetooth, and external storage (e.g., microSD cards), are mapped to Linux Group IDs. For instance, all applications with Internet permission become members of a Linux user group that has rights to create and access Internet sockets. In addition, recent Android builds ship with support for Security Enhanced Linux to further strengthen Android's security model (see Section 3.3).

MSSF also utilizes a combination of permissions and Linux access control. Applications communicate through D-Bus and local socket interfaces. Developers declare access control policies for inter-process calls using permissions and Linux access control mechanisms. MSSF access control policies can also be declared for file access. For example, a developer may define the permissions needed to access any of the files created by the application.

Java ME and Windows Phone platforms do not support third-party inter-process communication, and thus access control policy declaration does not apply to third-party software components. Access to system APIs is controlled with permissions.

4.1.5   ACCESS CONTROL GRANULARITY

The number of permissions, and thus the granularity of possible access control policies, varies between platforms. Both Symbian and Windows Phone utilize a coarse-grained model with a fixed set of permissions. 21 Symbian permissions are divided into four categories: User permissions can be granted by the user during application installation, System permissions require application signing by a trusted authority, Restricted permissions require application signing and stronger application developer identity verification, while Manufacturer permissions are reserved for device manufacturers. Windows Phone uses 16 permissions. Most permissions are granted by the Windows Phone marketplace, while device location permission requires additional user acceptance at installation.

Java ME, Android, and MSSF support a more fine-grained permission model. In Android and MSSF, third-party developers may define their own permissions. Java ME permissions are mapped into categories that are called *function groups*. The purpose of these categories is to present permission prompts to the user in an understandable format. The Java ME specifications recommend 15 function groups [100], but device manufacturers are allowed to defined their own groups.

The Android default permission set includes more than one hundred permissions, and developers are allowed to define their own permissions. Permissions are divided into four categories that are called *protection levels*: Normal, Dangerous, Signature, and SignatureOrSystem. All permissions require explicit user approval during the installation process. Dangerous, Signature, and SignatureOrSystem level permissions are presented more prominently to the user than Normal permissions. MSSF permissions are not categorized and developers can define their own permissions.

Starting from iOS version 6, Apple allows end-users to set privacy-related permissions on a per-app basis. Specifically, the privacy permissions cover access to location information, calendar, contacts, reminders, photos, microphone recording, and bluetooth sharing. Furthermore, one can restrict third-party apps from accessing the user's Facebook and Twitter account, and users can limit and even completely disable tracking by advertisement libraries. In contrast to Android, where permissions are fixed at install-time and cannot be modified afterwards, iOS allows users to change the permission settings for each app at any time. On the other hand, Apple only provides permission settings that concern the user's privacy.

4.2   APPLICATION INSTALLATION

In this section we compare application installation mechanisms. Table 4.2 provides a summary.

Table 4.2: Comparison of application installation security mechanisms

	Java ME	Symbian	Android	iOS	MSSF	WP
permission assignment	trusted authority, user at runtime	central authority, user at installation	user at installation	pre-defined profile	trusted authority	central authority
permission presentation	permission groups	permission names	permission groups	permission names	permission names	permission names
application update	same-origin policy, user approval	central authority, any developer	same-origin policy	central authority	trust level of marketplace	central authority

4.2.1   PERMISSION ASSIGNMENT

The installer assigns permissions to applications either based on application signing by a trusted authority or user approval during installation. Additionally, permissions may be assigned at runtime with user prompts. In Symbian permission assignment requires application signing by a central trusted authority if System, Restricted, or Manufacturer permissions are requested. If only User permissions are needed, the user can grant these permissions during installation.

Similarly, the Java ME platform utilizes permission assignment model that combines code signing by a trusted authority with user approval. Some permissions must be granted with code signing by a signing authority (e.g., mobile operator), while other permission-protected system API calls trigger runtime user prompts. These prompts are presented in terms of permission groups. If the user grants the requested permission, the decision applies to all permissions of the same group. The user can grant permissions to applications permanently, for application execution duration, or for one-time API call access.

In Android all permissions have to be approved by the user at installation time.[1] Permissions of Signature category can be given to an application only if it is signed by the same key as the application that declared the permission. SystemOrSignature permissions are similar to Signature permissions but additionally can be granted to applications trusted by the platform provider, i.e., applications which are installed on the default read-only system partition. In Android, multiple applications can share the same Linux user ID (UID). Since permissions are assigned on the granularity of application user IDs, applications sharing the same UID share their permissions. Sharing UIDs requires explicit developer approval, since all applications sharing a UID must be signed with the same developer key.

In MSSF, the marketplace provider specific policies control the permissions that each provider is allowed to grant. The installer assigns applications an intersection of the developer requested permissions and the marketplace supported permissions. All iOS applications are assigned to a pre-defined permission profile. However, access to certain system services, such as

---

[1]According to Android documentation [64], the installer can grant Normal permissions without explicit user approval. In recent Android implementations, Normal permissions are hidden from the permission list that is shown to the user at the time of installation. To see, and approve, Normal permissions the user has to explicitly expand the list.

location, has to be approved by the user explicitly at runtime. Since iOS 6 these checks have been extended, and applications now need the user's approval for privacy-related access requests to contacts, reminders, photos, Twitter and Facebook accounts, bluetooth sharing, microphone, and to calendar entries. The user's decision is centrally stored on the device to avoid asking the user for each access request. Nevertheless, iOS users have the possibility of modifying their privacy decision by using the system settings app.

Windows Phone permissions are assigned by the marketplace during the application distribution and shown to the user at the time of installation. The location permission is an exception: it requires explicit user approval.

4.2.2   PERMISSION PRESENTATION

Two basic approaches for permission presentation are used. In Symbian and Windows Phone, permission names are shown to the user. Both of these platforms are based on a coarse-grained permission model. On platforms with fine-grained permissions, group names are typically shown to the user. The Android platform shows permission group names to the user at the time of application installation, while Java ME generates runtime permission prompts using permission group names.

In iOS, only specific system API calls generate runtime prompts, and thus permission grouping is not needed. MSSF permissions are not shown to the user during installation or at runtime.

4.2.3   APPLICATION UPDATES

Update of a signed Java ME application is allowed only if the new application version is signed by the same trusted authority as the previous version (same-origin policy). When a signed Java ME application is updated, the application persistent storage is retained. In unsigned application update, the user is asked if the new application should have access to the persistent storage of the old version.

Symbian applications with an application identifier from the protected range can only be updated by an installation package that has been assigned the same identifier by the central trusted authority. Applications with an identifier from the unprotected range may be updated by any installation package.

In Android, application update is based on the same-origin policy. An application can be updated only from an installation package that is signed with the same developer key as the previous version. The updated application gets access to the data storage of the previous version by assigning them the same Linux UID.

MSSF applications can be updated if the installation package is signed by the same marketplace operator, or by another marketplace operator that has a higher trust level. The updated application gets access to the data of the previous application version. iOS and Windows Phone application updates are subject to application signing by the central trusted authority.

Table 4.3: Comparison of runtime protection mechanisms

	Java ME	**Symbian**	**Android**	**iOS**	**MSSF**	**WP**
runtime permissions	increase by user approval	constant	constant (with exceptions)	increase by user approval	increase by plugin loading, decrease on request	constant
access control enforcement	reference monitor	reference monitor, callee	reference monitor, callee, Linux DAC	reference monitor	reference monitor, callee, Linux DAC	reference monitor
execution protection	n/a	process isolation	NX bit, ASLR	NX bit, ASLR, CSE	ASLR	ASLR
application data protection	dedicated database	dedicated directory	dedicated directory and Linux access control	dedicated directory	permission-based policies	VM sandboxing
hardware security APIs	secure storage (JSR 177)	secure storage (proprietary)	secure storage (proprietary)	secure storage (file system, proprietary)	secure storage (file system)	n/a

4.3 RUNTIME PROTECTION

In this section we compare mobile platform runtime protection mechanisms. Table 4.3 shows a summary. Many of the security mechanisms discussed in this section (access control enforcement, execution protection, application data protection) fall under the broad definition of *sandboxing*. Typically, the term sandboxing refers to isolation techniques that on the one hand protect application execution and its data from being compromised by other concurrent applications. On the other hand, the same term also covers security mechanisms that ensure that each application can only perform authorized operations on the device. For example, an application must not be able to arbitrarily use all system resources and OS services, but only those that have been specified in the application manifest or system-wide sandboxing profile. The compared mobile platforms support different sandboxing enforcements, and also implement sandboxing at different layers in the software stack. Our comparison in this section will highlight these differences.

4.3.1 RUNTIME PERMISSIONS

In Symbian, developers request, and the installer assigns, permissions for shared libraries. Library loading fails, if the library does not have a superset of the application permissions. Pre-installed Symbian system libraries are typically assigned all permissions that third-party applications need. Once an application has been loaded, its permission set remains unchanged during the application execution.

In Android, separate permissions are not assigned to libraries, and thus library loading does not change application permissions. In general, Android application permissions are constant during application runtime. An exception are so called *URI permissions* which applications can use to temporarily grant access to certain data stored in services (Content Providers) to other applications.

In MSSF, library loading does not modify application permissions, but loading may fail if a library has been signed by a software source (marketplace operator or developer) that cannot grant all the permissions of the application. In MSSF application permissions may change at runtime for two reasons. First, the application permissions can increase when a plugin is installed, if the plugin has additional permission compared to the application. The rationale for such runtime permission increase is that plugin-supporting applications do not have to request all possibly needed permissions. Second, MSSF applications can themselves instruct the kernel to drop some of their permissions at runtime. For example, an application may need certain permissions only for a setup phase that is performed on the first execution of the application. Such an application can drop permissions that are no longer needed, and thus limit the damage of a possible runtime compromise.

Java ME permissions can be granted by the user at runtime. Thus, the permission set of a Java ME application may increase after installation. In the iOS platform, applications are assigned to a pre-defined profile and users can grant access to certain system resources at runtime. Permissions of Windows Phone applications do not change after installation.

4.3.2 ACCESS CONTROL ENFORCEMENT

In the Java ME, iOS, and Windows Phone, permission enforcement is straightforward. The reference monitor either allows or denies system calls based on the permissions of the applications. Other platforms provide more elaborate access control enforcement schemes.

Symbian services can implement their own access control enforcement. Such access control policies may use application permissions, application identifiers, and application vendor identifiers. In Symbian, access control is enforced both by the reference monitor and third-party services. The reference monitor augments IPC calls with permission and identifier information to facilitate enforcement by services.

Access control enforcement in Android is split between the middleware level for IPC and the kernel-level for low-level resources. On the middleware-level, the ActivityManagerService component controls Binder inter-process communication based on access control policies defined in manifest files. For Android services, the manifest permissions are checked by Activity-ManagerService only during the start/bind operation which needs to be called to use the service. Afterwards, already bound service references can be forwarded between applications, and thus developers are required to implement programmatic permission checks on service function invocations. Application developers may integrate manual permission checks in their application components also to enable more fine-grained access control than what is possible with manifest permissions alone.

Applications that require access to low-level resources protected by permissions, such as Internet, Bluetooth, and system log interfaces, are mapped to specific Linux groups IDs, and applications belonging to these groups are allowed to access such OS resources. Access control enforcement for these permissions is handled by the access control mechanisms of the modified Android Linux kernel (i.e., legacy DAC).

MSSF applications can perform IPC calls via two channels. In the case of D-Bus calls, the D-Bus framework acts as the reference monitor. Permissions for Unix socket IPC calls are enforced by the operating system kernel. Also services can implement access control enforcement.

4.3.3   EXECUTION PROTECTION

Runtime attacks, such as buffer overflows, are a common attack vector. In a typical buffer overflow attack, the adversary modifies the program call stack return address by writing more data into a buffer than what has been allocated for it. The excessive data overflows the stack return address, and allows the attacker to modify the execution control flow, for example, into a memory segment that contains code injected by the attacker [7]. Return-into-libc [104] and return-oriented programming (ROP) [68] attacks allow arbitrary code execution without code injection, by reusing existing system libraries. Such attacks are well known in PC platforms, and are also applicable to mobile devices [78, 79, 84, 102].

Compiler extensions, like stack canaries [31], are supported by many operating systems to make overflow attacks more difficult. NX bit (Never eXecute) mechanism enforces that a memory page cannot be both writable and executable at the same time. This prevents adversary injected code execution, but not ROP attacks. Address space layout randomization (ASLR) modifies the base address of code segments, such as the stack, heap, and linked libraries. ASLR complicates return-oriented programming attacks (the adversary can only guess the start address of his target code), but does not fully prevent them. Memory disclosure attacks may allow an adversary to learn code segment addresses at runtime [128].

Android leverages NX bit and ASLR which randomizes the base address of the heap, native executables, and the linker for each run [107]. The randomization mechanism of Android has limitations. New application processes are created by the root Dalvik VM instance (Zygote) that forks itself, and thus all Android applications share the same, randomized memory layout. The randomization only changes when the device is rebooted. Thus, if an adversary learns the memory layout of one application, he can use the obtained addresses during ROP attacks on other applications as well.

The iOS platform supports NX bit and *code signing enforcement* (CSE). In CSE, application binary signatures are verified before every application execution. If iOS application binaries have been modified when the device is turned off, or if a process attempts to modify a code page at runtime, the program execution is aborted. CSE prevents code injection, but is incompatible with just-in-time compilers. Dynamic code signing entitlement allows privileged applications, like the browser, to generate code at runtime. Vulnerabilities have been found in the CSE mechanism [115]. iOS also supports ASLR, from version 4.3. If an iOS application is compiled as a position-independent executable (PIE) [32], the platform will randomize all code segments of the application (text, heap, stack, shared libraries). For non-PIE applications, only the base addresses of shared libraries and heap are randomized.

MSSF utilizes NX-bit support of the Linux kernel. ASLR is not enabled due to executable pre-linking. Windows Phone devices support ASLR [108]. Java ME is an application platform, not an operating system, and thus execution protection is based on Java virtual machine isolation (sandboxing) only. The execution protection in Symbian is limited to traditional process isolation mechanisms, like isolated memory areas for each process.

4.3.4 APPLICATION DATA PROTECTION

In Java ME, applications do not have direct access to the device file system. Instead, database APIs are provided for persistent storage. These databases are either private to one application or shared with all applications.

In Symbian, a dedicated file system directory (called *private directory*) is created for each application. The private directory can only be accessed by the owner application or a process with permissions that are reserved for the device manufacturer. Developers may define whether the contents of the application private directory should be included in external backups. The default policy is to exclude private directory contents from backups.

Each Android application has a dedicated file system directory protected using the standard Linux discretionary access control (legacy DAC) mechanisms, which are based on user IDs and group IDs. By default, files in this directory can be written and read only by the application itself. During file creation, the application may explicitly define that the created file should be readable or writable by other applications. Android backups made to Google cloud service are protected by Google account authentication.

MSSF supports application data protection with permissions. Application developers can define the permissions required for individual files and file operations in the manifest file. The default policy is that application files can only be accessed by the application itself. On other platforms, similar permission-based data sharing can be implemented using permissions and inter-process communication.

Each iOS application has only access to its own file system directory. Third-party application data are included to system backups. Backups can be encrypted with a user password. Windows Phone applications have dedicated private file system directories and database tables. Windows Phone does not provide a backup feature that would include third-party application data.

4.3.5 HARDWARE SECURITY APIS

Java ME provides data encryption services to third-party developers using secure elements, such as SIM cards [111]. Nokia Symbian devices have APIs for encryption and decryption using a hardware-resident key. Access to these APIs is controlled with permissions. The encryption key

Table 4.4: Comparison of platform management mechanisms

	Java ME	Symbian	Android	iOS	MSSF	WP
platform boot integrity	n/a	secure boot	vendor-specific	secure boot	secure boot, authenticated boot	secure boot
platform data integrity	virtual machine isolation	dedi-cated directory	Linux access control, UID-based sandboxing	dedicated directory, CSE	Linux AC, Smack, IMA [121], EVM [132]	virtual machine isolation
system updates	n/a	central signing	central signing	central signing	multiple repositories	central signing
remote manage-ment	n/a	n/a	built-in features	built-in features	n/a	built-in features

is derived from the hardware-resident key and the application identifier to make the encryption application specific.

Android allows hardware-assisted data protection since version 4.3. Android applications can create hardware-protected key pairs using a standardized API and perform encryption and signature operations on them. The underlying implementation of hardware cryptography support is vendor dependent [65].

MSSF allows applications to encrypt data using a hardware key. Encryption key derivation is based on application identifier or specified permission which allows an application to encrypt data only for itself or to a set of applications. The encryption and decryption mechanism is integrated to the file system which allows legacy applications to benefit from offline data protection.

The iOS platform supports file encryption using a key that is derived from a hardware secret [9]. Application developers may define a *protection class* for stored data items. Encryption keys on highest protection class are derived from the device secret and a device passcode (used for the device screen lock), and deleted from device memory when the device screen is locked to prevent data leakage if the device is lost or stolen. Encryption on lowest protection class is based on the device secret only. The encryption is integrated to normal file system operations. Windows Phone has no built-in hardware encryption support.

4.4 PLATFORM MANAGEMENT

In this section we compare platform management mechanisms. Table 4.4 presents a summary.

4.4.1 PLATFORM BOOT INTEGRITY

The correct behavior of platform security mechanisms relies on the integrity of the platform components, such as the application installer and the reference monitor. Execution protection techniques discussed in the previous section provide protection against runtime modifications of these platform components by malicious applications. Besides runtime attacks, adversaries with physical access to the device may attempt to modify system components when the device is turned off. Such offline attacks can be addressed with hardware-assisted secure boot and authenticated boot.

Symbian, iOS, and Windows Phone platforms support secure boot. The boot verifier platform component, typically implemented as part of the boot loader, verifies the integrity of the booted operating system image using certified reference values. Most Android device manufacturers intentionally allow custom operating system versions by third-party developers, and thus Android platform components can be modified offline. The integrity of the Java ME platform components can be verified using the security mechanisms of the underlying OS.

MSSF supports both secure boot and authenticated boot. The device can be booted to *normal mode*, with the official OS kernel image provided by the device manufacturer, or to *developer mode*, with custom kernel provided by any developer [117]. Integrity of each component of the boot sequence, starting from the boot loader, is verified with signatures and reference values. However, if the integrity verification of the operating system image fails, the boot process is not halted, but the user is notified and asked permission to continue the boot. If the user decides to continue, this information is stored into an integrity-protected hardware register. When the OS requests access to device resources, such as hardware keys, the access can be controlled based on the mode of the device. Both modes allow applications to utilize hardware-assisted secure storage. The encryption keys are derived from a device-specific key and the mode of the device to prevent content encrypted in the normal mode from being decrypted in the developer mode.

4.4.2   PLATFORM DATA INTEGRITY

In addition to platform software components, also platform data, including the installed application code, the permission database and the policy database, need protection both from runtime attacks and simple offline attacks like modification of installed application executables stored on device internal persistent storage or removable media. Typically, techniques that are used for application data protection and execution protection can be used for platform data protection as well.

Java ME applications do not have direct access to the file system which prevents runtime platform data modifications by malicious applications. The Java ME platform security architecture does not address offline attacks or modifications of applications on removable media.

In Symbian, executable files are kept in, and exclusively loaded from, a dedicated directory in the device internal memory. Only processes with manufacturer permissions are allowed to access this directory. Symbian supports application installation to removable memory elements. In this case, the installer stores a hash of application executable to the device internal memory. When an executable is loaded from the removable memory element, a hash of the loaded executable is compared to a reference value stored in internal memory to prevent loading of any executable modified since its installation. Symbian platform security model does not address offline modifications of platform data stored in device internal media.

Android applications are stored in a dedicated file system directory. Linux access control mechanisms prevent runtime platform data modifications by malicious applications, because Android applications cannot run with system user privileges. Android allows internal media elements, i.e., the user data partition where third-party applications and application private data are stored, to be encrypted with a key that is stored in device internal memory and encrypted with a key derived from the user password or lock screen pattern [38].

In MSSF, running third-party applications with system user privileges (all POSIX capabilities) is not explicitly prevented. Application developers may request such privileges in the manifest file. Because of this chosen model, Linux access control mechanisms are not sufficient to prevent platform data modifications by malicious applications. Instead, Smack mandatory access control kernel module labels application executables and data with application identifiers. Using these labels, the kernel module controls application access to their own files and platform resources. All executables and shared libraries are assigned a label that prevents the application from modifying its own code.

Offline integrity protection is provided by a combination of Integrity Measurement Architecture (IMA) [121] and Extended Validation Module (EVM) [132]. During application installation, a reference hash for each application file is calculated. The reference hash is stored in an extended Linux file system attribute. The IMA mechanism verifies this hash when a file is accessed. When a file is modified at runtime, the file system attribute is recalculated. Offline integrity of these file attributes is preserved by the EVM module that calculates and verifies a keyed message authentication code using a hardware-resident key.

iOS applications are encrypted and signed for persistent storage. The application signature prevents unauthorized altering of the application, both runtime and offline. Similar to other platforms, iOS ensures runtime integrity of application executables and platform data by constraining file operations of applications. Windows Phone applications are executed in a sandbox of a virtual machine and do not have direct access to the device file system which prevents them from accessing platform data at runtime. The Windows Phone architecture does not address offline platform data integrity.

4.4.3   PLATFORM UPDATES AND DEVICE MANAGEMENT

Platform updates are typically signed by a central trusted authority, the platform provider. In MSSF, system updates are handled via the application installer, and thus it is possible to deploy system updates from multiple authorized software repositories. Normally, all system updates would originate from a single root repository that has the highest trust level. With regards to the remote management the only available MeeGo device, Nokia N9, has an initial small set of features supported by the platform.

Symbian does not provide built-in support for device management, although third-party device management solutions have been deployed on top of Symbian. Both system updates and device management are outside the scope of Java ME platform. Android, iOS, and Windows

Phone platform have built-in device management features. We discuss enterprise device management extensions in more detail in Chapter 6.

4.5   DEVICE ROOTING

As previously discussed, most mobile device manufacturers and platform providers enforce restrictions with regards to the use of the mobile device. For instance, iOS only allows Apple-signed software to be executed and Windows Phone users can only run applications distributed over the central Microsoft marketplace. Android users can install applications from any source, but they cannot modify the operating system configuration or run third-party applications (that have not been authorized by the device manufacturer) with system permissions by default.

Users may have various reasons for overcoming such restrictions, ranging from adding new system functionality such as ad blocking or firewall features to installing pirated software. To circumvent these device manufacturer and platform provider restrictions, users may opt to *jailbreak* or *root* their device. The notion of jailbreaking is typically applied to iOS devices, while the term rooting is more often used in the context of Android and other mobile platforms. By a common definition, the term rooting denotes to running third-party software on the device with root user identity and thus all possible system permissions. A common definition of jailbreaking includes overcoming the technical restrictions that limit application installation in addition to running arbitrary third-party software with system permissions. Device *unlocking* refers to the process of overcoming the restrictions of some mobile devices that allow users to only connect to one specific wireless network carrier.

Rooting and jailbreaking mobile devices has also disadvantages. Such procedures may void the device warranty, although typically rooting is not per-se illegal. Moreover, a failed rooting operation (e.g., a failed device flashing operation) may turn the device inoperable. Finally, malware distribution becomes easier after a jailbreak, as applications from any software source with any permissions may be installed.

4.5.1   IOS

The iOS jailbreak process is described in detail at various online sources (see, e.g., [130]). Here we give a summary: the jailbreak process typically requires connecting an iOS device to a computer and running jailbreak tools, such as *redsn0w* [5]. These tools guide the user through the jailbreak process and in most cases require him to interact with the device (e.g., pressing a button on the device screen). iOS jailbreaks can be divided into two categories. *Tethered* jailbreaks require a connection to a computer whenever the iOS device is rebooted. In an *untethered* jailbreak no such connection is needed except the time the initial jailbreak is launched.

As the iOS platform enforces signature checks on each executable along the boot process, one needs to bypass these signature checks in order to modify the operating system for jailbreaking. In general, there are two exploitation techniques: (i) a boot-time *bootrom* exploit or (ii) a runtime exploit at the application layer. Bootrom code is the first code executed when an iOS device is launched and also serves as the root of trust for measurement (CRTM). A vulnerability in the bootrom code allows an adversary to disable all signature checks and patch the device's firmware. As the vulnerability exists in bootrom code that is stored on read-only memory, such exploits can be addressed only by new hardware generations. In practice, bootrom exploits are rare, the last bootrom exploit (*limera1n*) dates back to 2010. Newer generations of iOS devices have not been found vulnerable to bootrom jailbreak exploits.

Application-level jailbreak exploits are more common. These exploits typically involve a chain of attacks from the application-level to the iOS kernel. After successful exploitation, the signature verification routines will always return true even for code that is not signed by Apple. For untethered jailbreaks, parts of the exploits have to be repeated at each reboot. Some of these jailbreaks do not require a connection to a PC. One prominent example is the *JailbreakMe* exploit, where a user only needs to download a malicious PDF file [93]. In contrast to bootrom exploits, application-level jailbreaks can be patched by a software update.

4.5.2 ANDROID

Rooting an Android device allows applications to execute functionality in the context of the root user (UID=0). A common approach to root an Android device is to place the Unix *su* tool on the *system* partition of the device. The purpose of *su* is to execute programs in the context of another user identifier at runtime. The owner of the *su* binary is set to the root user and the *setuid* bit is enabled. Furthermore, the file system access rights are set so that any UID on the system is allowed to execute the *su* binary. The setuid bit causes the *su* binary to be executed in the context of its owner, which is the root user. It thus allows applications to elevate their privileges to those of the root user. The *su* binary has to be placed on a partition which allows the execution of binaries with the setuid bit enabled, which is not the case for the *data* partition to which normal Android applications can write.

One common option is to temporarily replace the installed recovery system image with a modified version [27]. The recovery system is a minimal Linux-based operating system which is booted when a certain button combination is held when the device is powered on. It is usually used to reset the device to factory settings or to upgrade the Android operating system to a new version. The modified recovery system mounts the system partition and installs the *su* binary on it. This option is, however, only feasible if the boot loader of the device does not enforce secure boot, since otherwise it will not boot the custom recovery system. Another option is to exploit a vulnerable system service or the kernel to temporarily elevate the privileges of an application to root privileges. The application then proceeds to install the *su* binary inside the system partition.

Rooting an Android-device is a device-specific process which usually voids the vendor warranty. Because giving arbitrary applications root privileges is a security risk, developers have created tools for access control on this process. A modified *su* tool can be used, which communicates at runtime with an additional Android application (e.g., SuperSU [28]). This application queries the device user for consent whenever an application wants to elevate its privileges.

4.5.3 OTHER MOBILE OPERATING SYSTEMS

While most of the jailbreak and rooting tools are for iOS and Android, similar tools are available for other platforms as well. Additionally, some platforms provide built-in features enabling the use cases that motivates users to perform the jailbreak or rooting. A number of hacking tools have been reported for the Symbian OS [21]. For example, HelloOX2 application [22] reportedly installs a new root certificate to a Symbian device, and thus enables application sideloading.

N9 MeeGo device has a setting that allows application installation from arbitrary software sources. The user only has to accept the prompt that such installations are at his own risk. *Developer mode* setting in N9 allows obtaining the root privileges on the device and enables easy development on the platform [105]. An open mode kernel is available together with the flashing instructions [80].

Windows Phone provides a way to perform a developer phone registration that allows sideloading of applications [97]. This option requires an official developer registration. Additional Windows Phone jailbreaking tools have been reported [69].

CHAPTER 5

Mobile Hardware Security

As a part of the platform security model description in Chapter 2, we identified two types of hardware security functionalities. First, security mechanisms that are needed by the software-based platform security architecture: platform boot integrity and secure storage. Second, hardware security services that can be used by applications: device identification, isolated execution, and device authentication. In this chapter, we describe these hardware security mechanisms in more detail.

Figure 5.1 illustrates *trust anchors* (hardware elements, executable code, and external data) that are needed to implement these mechanism. We start our discussion with platform integrity, and continue to device identification, secure storage, isolated execution, and device authentication. We use a distinct font whenever we first introduce a concept illustrated in Figure 5.1. Finally, we discuss existing architectures and emerging standards for deployment of hardware security mechanisms in mobile devices.

5.1 PLATFORM BOOT INTEGRITY

5.1.1 SECURE BOOT

Many mobile device manufacturers verify the integrity of their platform components during the device boot. In a *secure boot* process, the device start-up is stopped if any of the platform components has been modified. A typical approach to implement secure boot is to make the beginning of the boot sequence immutable. A simple way to achieve immutability is to store the boot code sequence into a read-only memory (ROM) of the application-specific integrated circuit (ASIC) during mobile device manufacturing. The processor must unconditionally start executing from that memory area. A device manufacturer must also issue a set of boot code certificates that contain hashes of boot code. These certificates are signed with respect to a device verification root that should be also immutable on the device. A typical verification root is a hash of the device manufacturer public key [133, 134]. The verification root is usually shared within a family of manufactured devices, such as all devices belonging to a certain model.

Additionally, the mobile device hardware must be enhanced with a cryptographic mechanism that validates the signature of the first executed system component. The first component is typically a boot loader that further validates and executes the next executed platform component, for example, the OS kernel. If any of these platform component signature validation steps fail, the boot process aborts. The mobile device must ensure the integrity of the cryptographic mechanism. A typical way to achieve such integrity is to store the needed cryptographic algorithms on ROM.

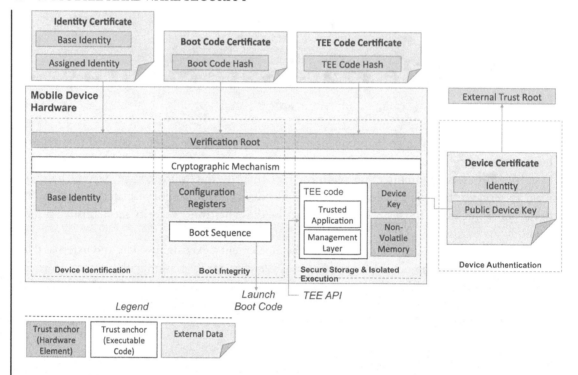

Figure 5.1: Mobile hardware-security mechanisms.

Secure boot with code signing does not necessarily imply that only a single platform version can be started on a given device. Instead, the launched platform code may be one of several certified alternatives. The booted platform version may depend on user selection, or other external or internal context. Besides verification of platform software components (i.e., executable code), similar verification can be performed on any configuration data whose integrity needs to be validated to guarantee the correct operation of the platform.

5.1.2   AUTHENTICATED BOOT

In contrast to secure boot, *authenticated boot* permits any platform component to be booted. During the boot process, measurements of booted system software, or aggregates of such measurements, are stored on hardware-based configuration registers. The boot loader measures the first loaded system component which in turn will measure the next component before launching it. The integrity of the configuration registers must be guaranteed during device runtime, an adversary must not be able to revert these registers into their previous state when the device is running. Offline persistence of configuration registers (i.e., integrity across boot cycles) is not needed for authenticated boot.

After the device boot, the stored values in the configuration registers determine the state of the platform components that were launched. This state information may include measurements from both executable code and configuration data. The booted system state can be used for two purposes. First, local access control enforcement regarding system resources like hardware keys can be based on the configuration register state. We describe such hardware mechanisms in Section 5.3. Second, a signed statement of the booted system state may be reported to an external verifier, as explained in Section 5.5.

5.2   SECURE STORAGE

Both the mobile platform and the third-party applications need secure storage. Secure storage can be divided into two security services: data integrity protection and data confidentiality protection. The platform data must be integrity protected, while many third-party applications require data confidentiality.

A pre-requisite of hardware-assisted secure storage is a persistent device key. The device key is immutable, typically device-specific, and accessible only to authorized software and hardware components. The device key may be initialized during ASIC manufacturing by storing it in a protected ROM area. Adversaries must not be able to read this memory area. To achieve such confidentiality, and to prevent simple memory bus attacks that are possible with external memory elements, the device key is typically stored in on the processor chip. Such memory elements are often called *on-chip memory*. Apart from the protected device key, the cryptographic algorithms needed for implementing secure storage, such as an authenticated encryption scheme, need integrity protection, both during storage and at runtime. Storage integrity can be implemented by storing such algorithms on ROM. Runtime integrity can be achieved by executing the cryptographic algorithm in isolation from the untrusted software components.

For data that requires both integrity and confidentiality, authenticated encryption algorithms can be used. For data items that require only integrity, a message authentication code (MAC) is sufficient. The hardware mechanism can calculate authenticators (often denoted as *tags*) over or encrypt data items that are stored on untrusted storage. For application-specific encryption, the encryption key can be derived by diversifying the device key using the identifier of the application requesting the encryption service, to prevent one application from decrypting data encrypted by another. Similarly, key diversification can be based on application group identifiers. The application identifiers are provided to the cryptographic mechanism by the platform, and thus integrity of the mobile platform is required to isolate application-specific encryptions from one another. As the resulting ciphertext and authenticators can be stored on any storage, the amount of data that can be integrity and confidentiality protected is not limited.

Besides authentication, some applications require *rollback protection*. A digital rights management application that controls the number of times certain content can be consumed, and a platform device lock mechanism that controls the number of PIN code attempts, are examples of applications in which the adversary should not be able to revert the stored application or platform data back into a previous, authenticated state. A simple way to achieve data rollback protection is to include non-volatile memory into the device hardware configuration. The non-volatile memory can be used to implement monotonically increasing counters. Counter values can be bound to data authenticators to prevent rollback. The non-volatile memory should persist its state across device boots.

5.3 ISOLATED EXECUTION

Applications, such as payment services and credit card implementations, should be executed in isolation from untrusted software components. While modern mobile operating systems and platforms are hardened against buffer overflows and other types of common runtime attacks, exploitable vulnerabilities are still possible. In general, software-based isolation mechanisms do not provide sufficient protection for applications with high security requirements.

The secure storage mechanism described previously allows execution of pre-defined cryptographic functionality (e.g., an encryption algorithm) in isolation from the rest of the system. While encryption and decryption, and a few additional common cryptographic operations such as signature calculation and verification, are sufficient for implementation of many applications, certain security services require isolated execution of application-specific algorithms that cannot be pre-installed on the device. For example, many online banking authentication systems require secure execution of one-time password algorithms. These algorithms are often vendor-specific and proprietary. To allow isolated execution of application-specific security algorithms, the mobile device hardware must support isolated execution of *arbitrary* code. The processing, memory, and storage capabilities needed for such isolated execution are called *trusted execution environment* (TEE).

To extend the secure storage mechanism described above for isolated execution of arbitrary code, the device hardware configuration must provide an interface (TEE API) through which the executable code (TEE code) can be loaded for isolated execution. If the TEE code uses only on-chip memory, it will resist simple physical attacks like tapping the memory bus between the processor chip and the main memory.

The executed TEE code has access to the device key, or a derivation of it, so that it can implement cryptographic operations using the key. To ensure that the code does not reveal the device key outside the trusted execution environment, either accidentally or by malice, the trustworthiness of the TEE code can be verified using code signing. A TEE code certificate that contains a hash of the TEE code, and is signed with respect to the device verification root, can authorize code execution within the trusted execution environment.

The TEE code can be structured using two types of software components. Trusted applications implement application-specific processing that needs to be isolated from the rest of the system. A TEE management layer provides a runtime execution environment for trusted applications and controls trusted application access to system resources like the device key. For example, using a management layer provided crypto API, trusted applications can apply cryptographic operations using a device-specific secret key to some data without ever directly accessing the key. The access that trusted applications have to the device key, and possibly to other similar hardware resources, can also be controlled based on platform state that is stored to configuration registers. For example, access to device key may be allowed only if the configuration registers show that a pre-approved platform version has been booted.

5.4   DEVICE IDENTIFICATION

Mobile devices need identifiers for several purposes. Regulators require that each mobile device should be assigned a unique and immutable identifier, the IMEI number. Additionally, device identifiers are needed for MAC addresses of local wireless interfaces. Immutability of the device identifier can be achieved by storing them in ROM during manufacturing. The ability to assign additional device identities after the ASIC manufacturing, rather than to fixing all of them into ROM at the time of manufacturing, gives more flexibility to the device manufacturers and integrators.

The combination of a verification root and at least one immutable base identity allows device manufacturers to assign arbitrarily many other identities to a chosen device. One way to achieve this is to issue an identity certificate for the device. The identity certificate is signed with respect to the verification root and it binds an assigned identity to the base identity. A trustworthy cryptographic mechanism is needed to verify the identity certificate, or a chain of such certificates.

5.5   DEVICE AUTHENTICATION

All security mechanisms described in this chapter thus far provide local security enforcements on a mobile device. Many security applications require communication with external entities. For example, platform providers want to verify the identity of a device during online service enrollment, while service providers like banks want to ensure that the device originates from a trusted manufacturer before provisioning keys, such as online banking credentials, to the TEE of the device. Device authentication can provide externally verifiable statements about the device identity, boot state, code executed on the device, and computation results. Such externally verifiable statements on device software configuration are often called *remote attestation*.

Publicly verifiable device authentication requires an asymmetric key pair. The key pair can be derived from the device-specific key, and the public part of the key pair can be certified during the mobile device manufacturing. A device certificate binds the device identity to the public part of the device key. The device certificate is signed typically by the device manufacturer, and can be verified with respect to an external trust root, such as the public key of the device manufacturer certification authority.

Additionally, the cryptographic mechanism on the mobile device hardware configuration must provide a signing algorithm that can be utilized with the private part of the device key pair. An externally provided fresh nonce signed with the device key, and verified using the device

Table 5.1: Summary of hardware security mechanisms

Security mechanism	Trust anchors	External data	Applications
secure boot (platform integrity)	verification root, crypto mechanism, boot sequence	boot code certificate	platform code integrity verification
authenticated boot (platform integrity)	crypto mechanism, configuration registers	—	platform code measurement
device identification	base identity, verification root	identity certificate	theft detection, subsidy lock
secure storage	device key, crypto mechanism, non-volatile memory	—	platform data protection, application data protection
isolated execution	device key, crypto mechanism, TEE code, TEE API, verification root	TEE code certificate	application execution protection
device authentication	device key, crypto mechanism	device certificate	remote attestation, provisioning, service enrollment

certificate, provides device identity authentication. Signed statements on configuration register content provide externally verifiable evidence on booted platform components for remote attestation.

Table 5.1 summarizes the hardware security mechanisms discussed in this chapter.

5.6   HARDWARE SECURITY ARCHITECTURES

Mobile device hardware architectures that implement many of the above-described security mechanisms have existed for almost a decade. The currently widely deployed ARM TrustZone architecture [12, 13] and the previously available TI M-Shield architecture [133] are examples of mobile device hardware architectures that enable security mechanisms in commodity mobile devices. In the rest of this section we describe mobile hardware security implementation using ARM TrustZone as an example.

In a common mobile device hardware configuration, the device main processor, cellular modem, small amounts of ROM and RAM, some peripheral and interrupt controllers, and debug and trace ports are included in the main processing core of the device. Also, some peripherals, such as wireless communication elements, may be included on the same chip—there is currently a tendency in mobile device manufacturing industry to include increasingly many mobile device functionalities in the same ASIC. Such architectures are often called *system on a chip* (SoC). The on-chip hardware components are connected with an internal bus. Other mobile device components, such as the system main runtime memory, flash memory elements, the display, a possible keyboard, and antennas are typically implemented as external components. Such off-chip hardware elements are connected with an external device bus.

In the TrustZone architecture the device main processor execution can be divided into two states: *secure world* and *normal world*. The processor executes in one state at a time. The secure world is intended for the *trusted execution environment* (TEE) while the normal world runs the mobile OS and its applications. This normal world execution environment is referred as the *rich execution environment* (REE).

The designer of a mobile device hardware configuration defines the hardware components that are accessible in these two states. In an example configuration, access to on-chip elements is restricted to the secure world only, while the device main memory and user input and output interfaces are accessible in the normal world. If needed, the device main memory can be partitioned into two segments: one that is accessible in secure world and another that is accessible in normal world. Typically, the on-chip ROM is populated during device manufacturing to contain the base identity, device key, verification root, and the cryptographic algorithms, while the on-chip RAM is used for isolated execution at runtime.

The access control between different hardware elements is implemented by adding a specific *control flag* to the system bus communication. Hardware elements connected to the system bus can enforce access control based on the control flag, or alternatively dedicated access control hardware can be added between the system bus and hardware elements that are not aware of the control flag and TrustZone architecture. The switch from the secure world to the normal world is only possible via a special *secure monitor call* (SMC) instruction that provides a controlled transition from the less privileged state to the more privileged state. Interrupts also can be configured by the mobile device manufacturer. Predefined interrupts can trigger an automatic switch from the normal world to the secure world, and thus certain types of events can be always processed directly by trusted TEE code.

Hardware-security architectures like ARM TrustZone that are integrated in the main processing core of the device are sometimes referred to as *processor secure environments* (PSEs) [36]. Although such architectures have been deployed to many mobile devices for almost a decade, the usage of hardware security mechanisms by third-party developers has been limited. Traditionally, mobile device manufacturers and platform providers have enabled hardware security mechanisms only for their internal purposes, such as subsidy lock protection. Third-party developer APIs like the JSR 177 interface for Java ME applications [111] have enabled secure storage with secure elements. Recent versions of Android and iOS platforms provide hardware-assisted secure storage APIs for developers. Interfaces to other hardware-security mechanisms, like isolated execution and device authentication, have not been widely available to third-party developers.

5.7   TEE STANDARDS

Recently, credential systems that allow more extensive usage of mobile hardware-security mechanisms have started to appear. MobiCore [55] and On-board Credentials [86] frameworks enable deployment of TEE code by third-party developers in TrustZone-enabled devices. The Global Platform (GP) industry alliance [61] is currently standardizing APIs for development and usage of security services in processor secure environments.

Figure 5.2 illustrates a trusted execution environment architecture with Global Platform specified interfaces [59]. Third-party mobile applications use hardware-based security services

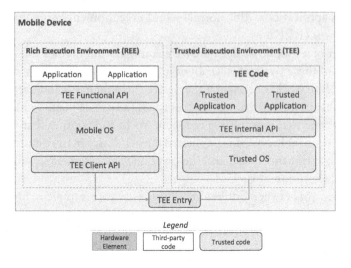

Figure 5.2: Global Platform trusted execution environment architecture [59].

using the TEE Functional API and the mobile operating system accesses the processor secure environment via the TEE Client API. Inside the TEE, trusted applications (TAs) are executed on top of a minimal execution environment called Trusted OS (TEE management layer). Trusted applications access device resources, such as cryptographic algorithms and keys, through the TEE Internal API. At the time of writing, the TEE Client API and the Internal API specifications are publicly available [57, 58], while the Functional API is still under development.

In addition to processor secure environments, the Global Platform specifications can be implemented using other types of security elements and environments. Removable security elements, like smart cards, on-chip security subsystems, and off-chip security co-processors are all possible ways of realizing the security mechanisms described in this chapter. The objective of the Global Platform standards is to define a set of common interfaces that allow easy development and usage of hardware-assisted security services across various mobile devices and TEE types.

The current Global Platform specifications do not define how trusted applications (i.e., TEE code) are provisioned to the TEE of a mobile devices. In smartcard systems, provisioning is a centrally controlled activity. A central trusted authority, called Trusted Service Manager (TSM), controls applications that can be installed to a set of smart cards of one issuer. The drawback of such *issuer-centric* provisioning model is that third-party developers cannot easily deploy hardware-assisted security solutions. Service deployment always requires a permission from, and possibly a business agreement with, a centralized authority.

A recent Global Platform white paper [60] promotes adoption of a *consumer-centric* provisioning model where the user of the mobile device is allowed to control which trusted applications can be installed into the TEE of his device. The On-board Credentials system has demonstrated feasibility of such open provisioning [37]. Adoption of the open provisioning model would allow easier deployment of hardware-assisted security services for third-party developers, and thus increase the innovation in mobile hardware security services. On the other hand, an open provisioning model implies more complicated credential life-cycle management. For example, user-friendly migration of previously provisioned credentials from one device to another is more difficult to realize if credentials originate from different independent issuers [85].

CHAPTER 6

Enterprise Security Extensions

Many commercial enterprise security extensions have been deployed to enhance the platform security mechanisms described in Chapter 2. These extensions modify different layers of the mobile platforms (OS kernel, middleware, application layer) to enforce security policies defined by an administrator. Security policies allow the administrator to define platform-specific rules the platform security architecture should enforce.

To achieve this goal, commercial platform security extensions focus on the following features. First, runtime device management features include lock screen policies, storage encryption, disabling components like camera and remote lock and wipe. Second, application management features include deployment of applications via enterprise application marketplaces, centralized application configuration, and application hardening. Third, isolated security domains for Bring Your Own Devices (BYOD) and dual-use scenarios. These platform security extensions are deployed on devices and are augmented by Mobile Device Management (MDM) solutions which enable administrators to administer and configure the specific features of the on-device security platform from the enterprise IT infrastructure.

6.1 ENTERPRISE SECURITY EXTENSION MODEL

Several components are involved in enterprise security extensions for mobile devices, as illustrated in Figure 6.1. These can be grouped into and infrastructure components (cf. Section 6.1.1) and on-device components (cf. Section 6.1.2).

6.1.1 INFRASTRUCTURE COMPONENTS

On the infrastructure side Mobile Device Management solutions integrate into standard infrastructure services, such as directory services, certificate authorities and enterprise groupware solutions for email and personal information management (PIM, e.g., calendar and contacts management). After an initial registration of the device with the Device Management Server, MDM solutions usually rely on platform-specific push messaging services to notify registered devices about policy updates. The Push Messaging Service is operated by the platform operating system manufacturer or MDM solution vendor and maintains a persistent connection to all registered devices.

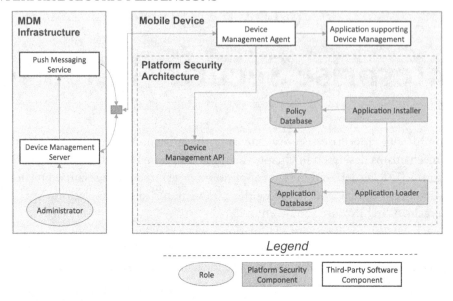

Figure 6.1: Generic MDM architecture.

6.1.2   ON-DEVICE COMPONENTS

On the device, three major components are involved in device management (see Figure 6.1).

Platform security architecture. The platform security architecture on the device enforces the security policy provided by the MDM solution. Different variants of security platforms exist, ranging from the stock platform security features (e.g., locking and wiping the device, setting lockscreen policies, enabling, and disabling hardware components or enabling, and disabling storage encryption) over application-based security solutions to sophisticated extensions which augment the stock platform-specific security features on the middleware and kernel level to provide enhanced device management features and access control on resources and isolated security domains.

Application-based approaches to security domain isolation consist of a (set of) applications which do not allow communication with other, non-trusted applications (see Figure 6.2(a)). These solutions rely on the platform software isolation and secure storage mechanism to isolate them and their respective data from the rest of the system. Based on the underlying security of the operating system, these solutions themselves implement access control to the sensitive resources they manage, for example, using application signature or identifier based whitelists. They are distributed using application marketplaces and thus can be installed without jailbreaking the device or installing a modified version of the operating system. For example, an application-based security domain for enterprises might consist of tightly

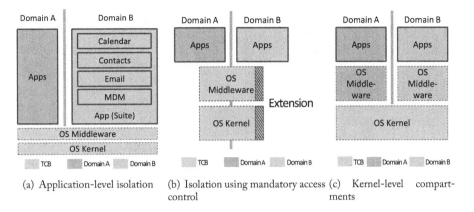

(a) Application-level isolation   (b) Isolation using mandatory access (c) Kernel-level compart-
                                  control   ments

Figure 6.2: Security domain isolation on application, middleware, and kernel level.

coupled groupware client for personal information management and email as well as other typical office applications, such as a word processor.

Solutions for the isolation of security domains on the system level can be categorized into three groups. First, isolation based on mandatory access control (MAC), which extends the access control enforcement points on the middleware and kernel level (see Figure 6.2(b)). Second, kernel-level compartments, which use the operating system's kernel namespacing mechanism to provide strictly or partially isolated userspace environments. And third, virtualization (see Figure 6.3) which provides two separate operating system software stacks on the device, either based on a Type-1 (also known as *bare-metal*) hypervisor which is directly executed on top of a minimal operating system or a Type-2 (also known as *hosted*) hypervisor which is executed on top of a rich host operating system. It should be noted that these solutions are not mutually exclusive but can be combined to further harden the security architecture.

MAC-based isolation requires the integration of a access control framework in the operating system kernel which cooperates with middleware MAC policy enforcement. While policy design is a hard problem, in addition to strict isolation solutions based on mandatory access control enable fine-grained unidirectional or bidirectional information flow between the domains. Depending on the implementation, the resource consumption of kernel-level compartments and virtualization may be problematic since large parts of code are executed in parallel. Memory deduplication and hardware-assisted virtualization may help to address these issues. Moreover, sharing data between the domains is cumbersome to implement using these approaches.

Mobile Device Management APIs. The previously described platform security architectures and compatible third-party apps can be remotely configured using a MDM API. Device and

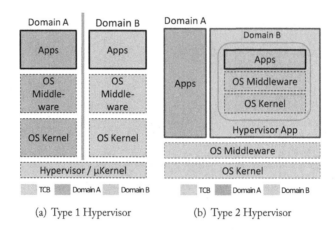

(a) Type 1 Hypervisor   (b) Type 2 Hypervisor

Figure 6.3: Security domain isolation using virtualization.

platform security solution manufacturers cooperate with selected MDM software vendors to better integrate their devices into MDM infrastructures.

Mobile Device Management Agent. MDM software agent deployed on the device communicates with the infrastructure components of the MDM architecture. First, the client enrolls the device based on user credentials (e.g., a username and password or an X.509 certificate). It then communicates with the Device Management API to configure the device to be compliant with the security policy defined by the administrator and waits for management commands. For communication, usually a combination of a push message service and a vendor-specific network protocol initiated by the agent on-demand (pull-mechanism) is used.

6.2   SELECTED COMMERCIAL SOLUTIONS

In this section we present a high-level overview of selected security solutions, focusing on the Android OS.

6.2.1   APPLICATION LEVEL EXTENSIONS

Both *Good for Enterprise* [62] and *Enterproid Divide*[77] provide an isolated suite of enterprise applications. Using Software Development Kits which enable third-party application developers to extend the specific solution and/or binary rewriting of common third party applications the administrator can extend the enterprise security domain with additional apps. Both solutions additionally integrate mobile device management features and allow the administrator to centrally manage the enterprise security domain and the device itself. Both solutions use a vendor-specific network operations center for communication with the devices.

6.2.2 PLATFORM LEVEL EXTENSIONS

Three Laws of Mobility (3LM) [6] and *Samsung SAFE* [124] are vendor-specific security extensions operating on the middleware and kernel level. They provide extended encryption features, e.g., file-based encryption of the removable storage area and integrate additional hooks for device runtime management into the stock Android OS. They extend the standard Android device management API with additional features, such as restricting which applications may or may not be installed on the device using blacklists or whitelists, application runtime permission management, remote VPN configuration, and central provisioning of cryptographic credentials.

BizzTrust [52] is a middleware and kernel-level extension which uses mandatory access control based on Security Enhanced Android (SEAndroid) [131] to implement isolated security domains. It integrates central device management and allows for the central administration of the enterprise security domain and the device. Information flow between the enterprise and the private security domain is strictly controlled on all layers of the Android operating system. *Samsung KNOX* [125] uses a similar approach to provide isolated security domains.

Cellrox Multi Persona Platform [26] and *trust|me* [51] are kernel-level security solutions which provide isolated userland security domains based on kernel-level containers. *Vmware Mobile Virtualization Platform* [16] and *Simko 3* [136] provide isolated security domains using virtualization. The former is a Type-2 Hypervisor which is executed on top of the normal Android OS, while the latter uses a L4 Microkernel on top of which multiple operating system instances are executed using paravirtualization.

6.2.3 MOBILE DEVICE MANAGEMENT SOFTWARE

MobileIron [101] offers solutions for mobile device management which comprise several infrastructure and client side components.[1] For device management, the MobileIron Virtual Smartphone Platform (VSP) server is used for central mobile device and application management on the infrastructure side. It communicates with the MobileIron Sentry server, a proxy between supported mobile apps and infrastructure services. For example, the Sentry can be used to limit access to a groupware server to policy-compliant devices.

On the client side, MobileIron uses the standard Android MDM interfaces and enforces device policies. Furthermore, additional policies for device- and vendor-specific extensions to the Android OS (e.g., Samsung SAFE) can be configured and deployed using MobileIron. The MobileIron agent on the local device logs suspicious behavior of the mobile device and notifies the MobileIron infrastructure whenever a policy violation, for example a jailbreak, is detected. The server in turn notifies the Administrator. Additionally, it notifies the Sentry server which in turn prohibits any further communication between supported applications on the mobile device and the services provided by the infrastructure until the device conforms to a policy-compliant state again.

---

[1]MobileIron VSP serves as an example of MDM solution. A comprehensive study of different MDM solutions [54] is out of the scope of this book.

CHAPTER 7

Platform Security Research

Recently, various security extensions have been proposed to tackle security and privacy issues of mobile devices. In general, the proposed solutions target different operating systems, platforms, and particularly different layers of the software stack. An abstract view of the different software layers a security extension may target is shown in Figure 7.1: (i) the operating system kernel, (ii) the middleware layer where the core mobile phone OS services reside, and (iii) the application layer with built-in and third-party user applications inside.

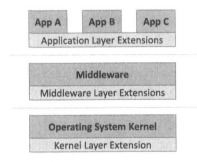

Figure 7.1: Security extensions for different layers.

Past research has mainly focused on Android due its popularity and openness. Hence, in this section, we mainly focus on platform security research targeting the Android OS (Section 7.1). Nevertheless, we also elaborate on recently published research result in the space of iOS security (Section 7.2).

7.1 ANDROID-BASED PLATFORM SECURITY RESEARCH

7.1.1 ATTACKS AND THREATS

Privilege Escalation

In general, privilege escalation attacks involve the exploitation of software and configuration flaws to elevate the privileges of an application. Thus, these attacks allow an application to perform operations and access data beyond its original authorizations. Applications on PC platforms executed by a single user typically share the same privileges. To extend the privileges of an application, most known attacks aim at exploiting a small number of higher-privileged daemons or services and the kernel to gain partial or full control over the system.

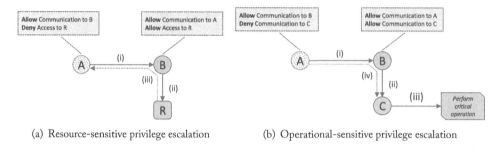

(a) Resource-sensitive privilege escalation   (b) Operational-sensitive privilege escalation

Figure 7.2: Basic principle of application-level privilege escalation attacks.

However, the situation on mobile operating systems (such as Android) is different, because each application is assigned a unique set of permissions to perform its task. This raised a new form of escalation attacks that we refer to as *application-level* privilege escalation attacks. In contrast to the aforementioned *kernel-level* privilege escalation attacks, these attacks aim at exploiting other user applications. A prominent example for such an attack is a privacy leak attack, where an application A is allowed to send text messages and a second application B can access the address book. When A exploits B, it can indirectly access contact data (although it has no permission to access this data), and transmit the retrieved information to an adversary via text messages.

An informal representation of such application-level privilege escalation attacks is shown in Figure 7.2, where we roughly distinguish between a resource- and an operational-sensitive privilege escalation attack. In both cases, a malicious application (denoted as A) exploits a configuration bug or an open interface of application B to either access a protected resource (Figure 7.2(a)) or to delude a third application C to perform a security-critical operation although application A has no permission to talk to C (Figure 7.2(b)). In a resource-sensitive attack an adversary may gain unauthorized access to SMS messages, contacts, mail, images, calender entries, or music files. In contrast, operational-sensitive attacks allow an application to trigger unauthorized actions, e.g., setting up a phone call, sending an SMS to high-premium rate number, or changing WiFi settings.

In most privilege escalation attacks, application B is considered as a benign but vulnerable application, e.g., it does not enforce a permission check when A accesses its interfaces. Such attacks are referred to as *confused deputy* attacks [72], where application B acts as a deputy for A, and is additionally confused because it does not check the privileges of A. In an alternative attack scenario, both application A and B are malicious and collaborate each other to merge their individual sets of permissions to jointly induce malicious behavior. These attacks are mainly referred to as *collusion* attacks [94, 127]. Compared to single malware attacks (where all necessary permissions have been requested by the malware developer to A), these attacks circumvent static secure installers (e.g., Kirin [43] in case of Android) because the dangerous combination of permissions has been divided over individual applications, and the static analysis checker does not consider the potential for two colluding applications for communication with each other to pool their privileges.

Malicious Applications

The popularity of smartphones along with the fact that these devices store a large amount of sensitive data (e.g., SMS, contacts, or calender entries), and feature charged services (e.g., phone calls, SMS, and MMS) have made them an appealing target of various malware attacks. The open application ecosystems (in particular that of Google Android) allows everyone to register as an app developer and upload arbitrary applications. This openness makes it very easy to upload and distribute malicious applications. For instance, in the first half of 2013 approximately 520,000 new Android malware strains have been recorded by G Data [19]. The malware may be distributed to the end-users through ad libraries, re-packaged apps on third-party Android markets, drive-by downloads, or botnets. The research community has addressed the threat of malware variously, e.g., by static and dynamic analysis of application binaries, enhanced application installers, novel run-time privacy frameworks, app store analysis tools, or security extensions that enforce access control for in-app advertisement libraries.

Risky In-App Ad Libraries

Many apps display to users advertisements in order to bring revenue to application developers. This is especially common for free apps, as their developers do not get any financial benefit from application purchase. To make use of advertising services, app developers integrate advertisement libraries (or ad libraries for short) as part of the application. When packed together, the hosting application and the ad library share privileges, which enables ad libraries to misuse privileges of host apps.

AdRisk was the first framework aimed at evaluating potential privacy and security risks by in-app ad libraries [67]. Researchers conducted a large-scale study on a set of 100,000 of Android apps and provided an in-depth analysis of 100 most popular ad libraries used by 52.1% of these apps. The security risks posed by ad libraries range from accessing private user data (e.g., the user's call logs, phone number, browser bookmarks, or even the list of apps installed on the phone) to deploying unsafe mechanisms to directly fetch and run code from the Internet. Further, in a follow-up work [129] researchers also identified a threat of ad service misuse by host apps, where the application pretends to show advertisements, while hiding them from the user and generating revenue for the developer.

7.1.2   SECURITY EXTENSIONS FOR ANDROID

Figure 7.3 gives a high-level overview of the main relevant security extensions proposed by the research community in the last few years for Android. We have categorized each solution into the Android architecture, such as the middleware layer (consisting of the application installer, reference monitor, permission database, and Dalvik virtual machine) and the Android Linux kernel.

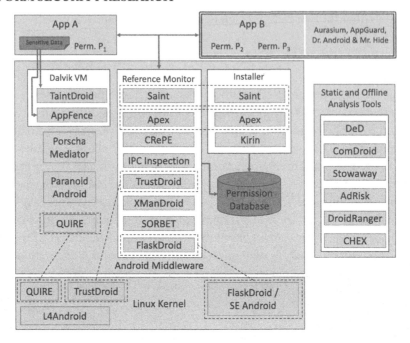

Figure 7.3: Main security extensions for Android.

Each solution requires extension to one or more components. Figure 7.3 also shows several offline static analysis tools that aim to detect vulnerable or malicious applications and interfaces.

In the remainder of this section we discuss each of the depicted solutions according to the security problems they aim to solve. We start with detection and prevention of privilege escalation. Afterwards, we elaborate on solutions that aim at detecting malicious applications, malicious advertisement libraries, and privacy leaks. We also describe frameworks to harden applications and their interfaces.

Frameworks to Mitigate Privilege Escalation
QUIRE (see Figure 7.4) is an Android security extension that provides a lightweight provenance system for IPC calls to prevent confused deputy attacks [34]. In order to determine the originator (provenance) of a security-critical operation, QUIRE tracks and records the call chain of IPC calls, and denies the request if the originating application has not been assigned the corresponding permission. Additionally, QUIRE extends the network module residing in the Android Linux kernel to perform its analysis also on remote procedure calls (RPCs). In summary, QUIRE addresses privilege escalation attacks that exploit vulnerable interfaces of trusted applications. However, QUIRE does not address privilege escalation that are based on maliciously colluding applications. Since the call chain is forwarded and propagated by the applications themselves,

colluding applications may forge the call chain to obscure the originating application, and hence, circumvent QUIRE's defense mechanism. Further, the current scheme of QUIRE is not transparent to applications; instead, application developers have to integrate QUIRE checks themselves.

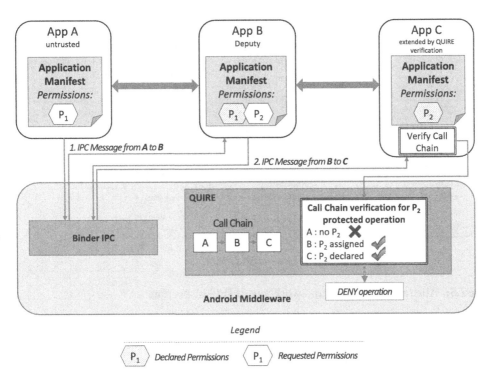

Figure 7.4: Abstract architecture and workflow of QUIRE.

Similar to QUIRE, **IPC Inspection** (see Figure 7.5) addresses confused deputy attacks [49]. Remarkably, the authors discovered several attacks against Android's system applications and demonstrated that a number of pre-installed applications in Android 2.2 are vulnerable to confused deputy attacks. For instance, every application can access the interface of the Settings application to change the WiFi, Bluetooth, or GPS settings without requiring the permission to change these settings. To tackle such confused deputy attacks, IPC Inspection creates a new application instance when an IPC call is delivered from a less-privileged application. Further, IPC inspection reduces the permission set of the receiver to the intersection of the permissions of the received and sender. One major benefit of IPC inspection resides in the fact that it does not require developers to define security policies to prevent privilege escalation attacks. However, IPC Inspection is likely to impose significant usability drawbacks and performance penalties, because it requires the creation and maintenance of multiple application instances with different sets of permissions.

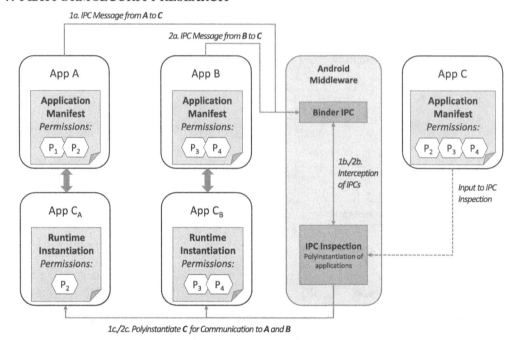

Figure 7.5: Abstract architecture and workflow of IPC inspection.

The **XManDroid** framework (see Figure 7.6) addresses both confused deputy and collusion attacks [120]. Specifically, it generates a system graph where nodes represent applications and edges the communication links among these applications. Based on a system-centric policy (which defines security-critical communication patterns), XManDroid checks at runtime whether a desired communication link should be allowed. In contrast to QUIRE or IPC Inspections, XManDroid does not only cover standard IPC communication, but also communication at the kernel-level through file reads/writes, and network sockets. Moreover, it detects collusion attacks that exploit side-channels over the Android's core application (e.g., Soundcomber [127]). On the other hand, it requires the definition of a policy that foresees all potential malicious communication patterns, that may lead to false positives.

Another system to prevent confused deputy attacks and undesired information flows is **SORBET**, a policy enforcement system which allows developers to use permissions to define secrecy and integrity policies [50]. In particular, the authors aim at setting up a formal framework for analyzing permission-based mobile operating systems. Using this framework, they demonstrate shortcomings of Android's design and implementation that allow privilege escalation attacks. For instance, Android's run-time delegation permissions (URIs—unified resource identifiers) suffers from several flaws such as the URI permissions are not properly revoked, and they can be delegated to other applications. To mitigate the threat of privilege escalation attacks, SORBET

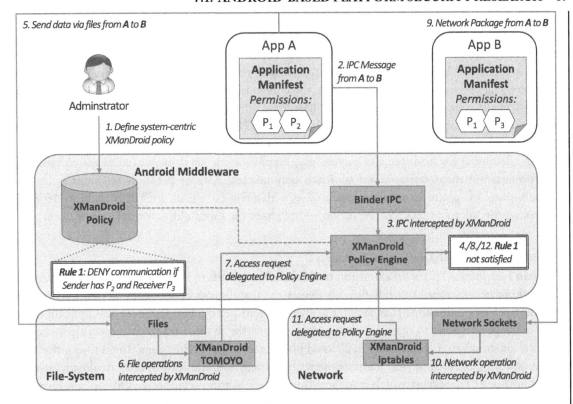

Figure 7.6: Abstract architecture and workflow of XManDroid.

allows a developer to define permission-based information flow policies in the Android manifest. These policies could, for instance, prevent an application from using dangerous permissions (e.g., INTERNET) after it has accessed a protected resource such as the address book (to prevent contacts leakage). However, SORBET cannot prevent privilege escalation attacks through colluding application, because it relies on developers to define the secrecy policies themselves.

Apart from defense techniques against privilege escalation attacks, several works have been proposed to tackle the problem of kernel-level privilege escalation attacks, i.e., attacks that aim to exploit a bug in the kernel to elevate the privileges of an application to root privileges. For instance, the Gingerbreak exploit (that has been discovered in several malware samples) acquires root privileges to install other packages and utilities [135]. One approach to tackle these attacks is to enable fine-grained access control at the kernel level by using the principle of SE Linux which has been very recently adapted to Android, called **SE Android** [106, 131]. Specifically, SE Android confines privileged Android system daemons, controls application interactions at kernel-level, and controls all access request to system resources. Alternatively to SELinux, the

XManDroid framework [120] deploys Tomoyo Linux [71] to enable access control at kernel-level.

A more general approach to tackle the problem of kernel-based attacks is the deployment of a secure microkernel which separates and isolates the operating system subsystems from each other using userspace processes, and from the core kernel functionality (e.g., IPC, memory management and scheduling). For instance, **L4Android** introduces a microkernel based on L4 that can execute underneath of the Android operating system [87]. In practice, L4Android is used in the SIMKO 3 architecture, which uses virtualization to separate multiple operating system instances (e.g., Android) for business and private use, cryptographic services, and network connectivity. However, this microkernel-based approach may not reach wide-spread deployment since most mobile and PC platform operating systems — with a few exceptions such as Blackberry 10 which deploys the microkernel QNX Neutrino — are based on a monolithic kernel architecture.

Security-Enhanced Application Installers

Kirin (see Figure 7.7) is an extension to Android's application installer [43]. Its model requires checking permissions at install-time. It denies the installation of applications that may encompass a set of permissions that violates a given system policy. For instance, an application that asks for permissions to read the phone state, record the audio, and open network connections is an indicator for a (potentially malicious) phone recording permissions. In addition, the Kirin framework described in [42] identifies security-critical communication links to already installed applications by analyzing which interfaces the new application is authorized to contact. However, Kirin is static and derives its decisions only based on the permissions requested by the application. Hence, it can only provide a vague indication whether an application is benign or could be malicious. Moreover, the system policy is likely to be incomplete, or either result in false alarms for applications that request a large number of permissions. A prominent example is the Skype App, which asks for almost every permission the Android system defines.

Another installer extension is **Apex**, which allows the user to selectively grant and deny permissions requested by applications at install time [92]. Moreover, the user has the possibility to define runtime constraints, e.g., limit the number of text messages to be send per day. Even though Apex makes Android much more flexible by allowing users to constraint certain functionalities, it unfortunately relies on the user to take security decisions. It also suffers from usability problems, because applications may unexpectedly terminate (crash) because they may not be able to handle a permission deny decision.

Privacy Frameworks

TaintDroid (see Figure 7.8) is an extension to the Android Dalvik virtual machine to detect unauthorized leakage of sensitive data [40]. For this, it exploits dynamic taint analysis in order to label privately declared data (such as location data, or contacts) with a taint mark, tracks tainted data as it propagates through the system, and alerts the user if tainted data is about to leave the

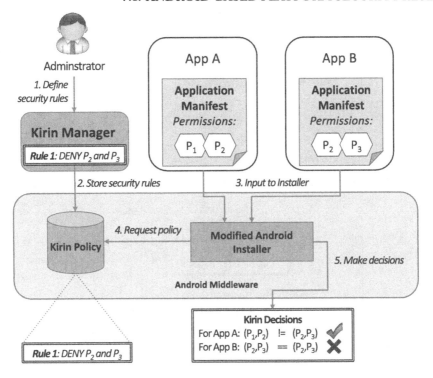

Figure 7.7: Abstract architecture and workflow of Kirin.

system at a taint sink (e.g., network interface). TaintDroid is able to detect data leakage attacks potentially initiated through a privilege escalation attack. However, TaintDroid mainly addresses data flows and does not cover control flows. Moreover, it does not monitor native code execution. The authors mention that tracking the control flow with TaintDroid will likely result in much higher performance penalties. In a follow-up work, Hornyack et al. introduced an application of TaintDroid called **AppFence** [75]. AppFence (see Figure 7.9) enforces the following mechanisms: (1) data exfiltration, i.e., allowing an application to access private data, but preventing it from leaking it to a remote server, and (2) data shadowing, which replaces private data with fake or shadow data for those applications that are not allowed to access private information. However, the problems of TaintDroid also apply to AppFence (e.g., native code is unmonitored and control-flows are not supported).

Another approach to mitigate attacks that threaten the user's privacy is **TISSA** [150]. Basically, TISSA consists of two parts, a user application that allows the user to specify privacy access rules on a per-application basis, and an extension to the Android middleware which enforces the privacy rules. The privacy rules cover location data, the phone ID, contacts and call logs, and for each of these the user can choose to allow access, return anonymized data, return fake data, or

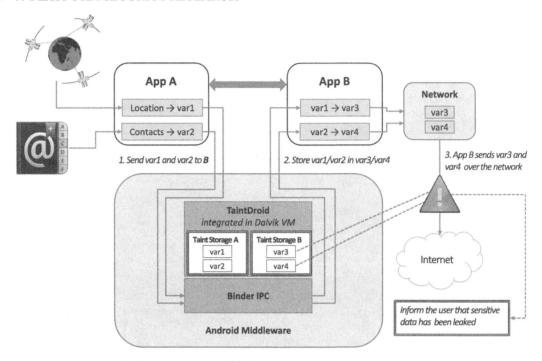

Figure 7.8: Abstract architecture and workflow of TaintDroid.

return an empty list. However, it is questionable whether a user is able to accurately decide about each app's privacy level.

Finally, **Porscha** provides policy-oriented secure content handling in Android. The goal of Porscha is to bind any security-sensitive data or content to a certain phone and to a specific set of applications. Content sources such as devices transmitting SMS, MMS, or e-mails can attach a DRM (Digital Rights Management) policy to the message. Even though Porscha introduces a much more fine-grained permission model, it cannot prevent leakage of data not tagged with a security policy [109].

Secure In-App Ad Libraries

Adsplit decouples host apps and in-app ad libraries and runs them as separate application instances with individual sets of permissions [129]. Moreover, the framework leverages mechanisms from Quire [34] to allow the remote server to verify if the advertisement was indeed displayed to the user. The tool provides automated means for decoupling the apps from their libraries and for determining the set of privileges necessary for each of them, which allows for easy application of the new concept to the existing apps. On the downside, it requires modifications to the underlying operating system.

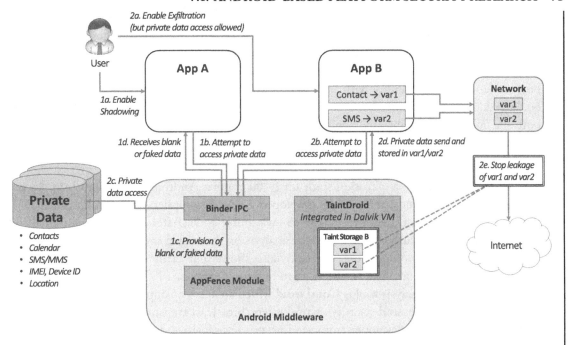

Figure 7.9: Abstract architecture and workflow of AppFence.

AdDroid is an alternative approach to isolate ad libraries from host applications [113]. It offers a dedicated system service which provides functionality typically found in ad libraries. Particularly, AdDroid introduces a new advertising API into Android OS and new permissions which have to be requested by apps requiring ad support. As a new service is a part of Android, AdDroid also requires relevant extensions to the underlying OS. Further, it is not straightforward for advertisers and app developers to move to a new service, as it would require appropriate changes in apps to adapt to new ad interfaces. Moreover, currently advertising networks are flexible in introducing arbitrary functionality to their libraries and can control library updates on their own, while approach taken by AdDroid would provide only well-defined functionality (although sufficient for most advertisers) and restrict functionality updates to Android release cycles. To mitigate these disadvantages, AdDroid does not preclude the use of the existing library-based model, but can co-exist with it.

Secure Embedding of UI elements
LayerCake [118] is a modified version of Android 4.2 which allows host applications to securely embed user interfaces (i.e., Activities) from other applications. The approach is conceptionally similar to embedded iframes in the context of web pages and can be used to split ad libraries from their host applications (cf. Section 7.1.2), to securely embed social networking buttons

(e.g., the Facebook "like" button) into applications or to implement user-driven access control systems [119], where access control decisions are derived directly from user intent at runtime. It furthermore can prevent clickjacking attacks where the user is tricked into clicking hidden UI elements in a malicious application (e.g., an ad hidden under a game's input button). Layercake provides limited compatibility with legacy applications: Activities from legacy applications may be embedded, but switching between multiple Activities of the embedded application requires both the host and the embedded application to adhere to their system model.

Static Analysis Tools

Enck et al. performed an application study on 1,100 popular Android applications [41]. To perform the application study, the authors developed a new decompiler for Android, called **DeD**. Basically, it decompiles Dalvik executables to Java source code. After obtaining the source code of the application, the authors perform static analysis on the source code to detect vulnerable interfaces and malicious components. The study also shows that many applications leak sensitive information like phone identifiers and location to remote servers.

Another static analysis tool is **ComDroid** which analyzes an application to detect vulnerable application interfaces and security-critical intent/broadcast transmissions [29]. For instance, it warns the application developer from sending privacy-sensitive data with a public broadcast, because this would allow a malicious registered broadcast receiver to eavesdrop the message. In a follow-up work, Felt et al. introduced a static analysis tool, called **Stowaway**, that is built on top of ComDroid and checks whether an application follows principle of least privilege [47]. In particular, the authors applied Stowaway to 940 Android applications and showed that one third of them are over-privileged, i.e., they ask for more permissions than they need to perform their operations.

CHEX is another static vetting tool for Android apps which particularly detects component hijacking vulnerabilities (including vulnerabilities that could be exploited by an adversary to launch a confused deputy attack) [91]. For this, it discovers all possible entry points of an application and performs data-flow analysis afterwards to detect such component hijacking vulnerabilities. In 5,400 Android apps CHEX discovered 254 potential component hijacking vulnerabilities (48 flagged apps were false positives; accuracy rate 81%).

The main problem of static analysis tools resides in the fact that they are likely to be incomplete, because they cannot completely predict the actual application behavior and communication patterns that will occur at runtime. In particular on Android, applications may use Java reflection to inspect classes and fields, as well as instantiating new objects at run-time. Moreover, an adversary can use obfuscation techniques to circumvent detection by the static analysis tools.

Dynamic Analysis Frameworks

To address the limitations of static analysis tools, several dynamic approaches have been proposed to detect malicious application behavior.

The **Paranoid** system detects viruses and runtime attacks by deploying a virus scanner and dynamic taint analysis [114]. However, the analysis is not performed on the user's device. Instead, Paranoid records the execution and transmits it to a remote analysis server, which then replays the execution and applies the aforementioned techniques. For this, Paranoid requires the execution trace to be stored in secure storage (in order to prevent malicious modification). Nevertheless, this impacts the device's performance and battery and only detects attacks after they have been already successfully launched.

Another dynamic analysis platform is **DroidScope** [145]. Basically, DroidScope deploys a virtualization-based analysis engine using QEMU [20] to detect malicious application behavior. In particular, it reconstructs the semantic view of the Android OS kernel and the Dalvik VM to allow offline but dynamic analysis of apps. Analysts can use an API to monitor native system calls, or Dalvik instructions. However, as soon as malware recognizes that it is currently emulated, it may use evasion techniques to destroy itself or obfuscate its malicious behavior from DroidScope.

App Store Analysis Tools

DroidRanger is the framework aimed for the detection of malicious apps in app markets [149]. It applies a heuristics-based filtering scheme to identify potentially risky apps based on the requested permissions or suspicious functionality such as dynamic code loading. Further, it performs in-depth analysis of risky apps and uses two techniques for the detection of known and zero-day malware: Behavioral footprint matching and dynamic execution monitoring, respectively. Behavioral footprint matching includes manual analysis of known malicious samples and deriving their behavioral footprint, such as listening to incoming SMS messages or using certain API calls. In the detection stage, static analysis is used to identify new malware instances matching the footprint. In contrast, dynamic execution monitoring includes runtime observation of the suspicious application and focuses on monitoring of security sensitive system calls (e.g., those that can be successfully executed only under root privileges). DroidRanger was evaluated on a large corpus of apps (more than 200 000 instances) from five different Android markets and effectively identified multiple instances of known and zero-day malware.

Several works introduce detection frameworks for identifying re-packaged smartphone apps on app markets [146, 147]. The problem was first introduced in, where the authors discovered that many smartphone apps get re-packaged (or re-signed) with goals to steal advertisement revenue from original app developers or to include malicious payloads targeting end users. The authors propose **DroidMOSS** for the detection of the re-packaged apps on third-party marketplaces [147]. DroidMOSS extracts application code and extracts code fingerprint by applying a fuzzy hashing technique [76] to detect similar code base of the original and re-packaged app. The authors apply their framework to 22,906 apps collected from 6 third-party marketplaces and identified that 5–13% of them are re-packaged copies of apps hosted at the official Android market.

The follow-up work presents a framework called **PiggyApp**, an improved solution for detection of re-packaged apps [146]. The authors introduce a new approach for detection of such apps: decoupling technique to extract the main application functionality, and an efficient feature fingerprint technique to detect apps with similar main part. In contrast to DroidMoss, PiggyApp framework is applicable for detection of re-packaged apps on both, the official and third-party app markets. Further, the algorithm complexity is reduced from $O(n^2)$ in the previous work to $O(n * log n)$, allowing for a large-scale analysis.

Barrera et al. emphasize advantages of centralized application markets with regards to security, such as a central point for malware detection, application ranking, and kill switches and point out that multi-market environments undermine effectiveness of these security mechanisms [17]. They propose **Meteor**, the security-enhanced application installation framework that relies on multiple server-side components such as market independent application databases, developer registers, and multiple kill switch authorities for bridging the gap between non-cooperating app markets. Unfortunately, maintaining multiple market independent server-based components might be difficult in practice, as it is not clear which entities could maintain these services, and how to establish trust in them (e.g., to prevent adversaries from running rogue kill switch authorities and killing security relevant apps such as anti-virus scanners).

Application Hardening

SAINT (see Figure 7.10) introduces a fine-grained access control model that allows applications to protect themselves from being misused and exploited [110]. Basically, it requires application developers to specify security policies to their applications. Moreover, it extends the basic Android OS to allow the system to enforce security decisions based on signatures, configurations, and contexts (e.g., phone state or location), whereas security decisions are enforced both at install-time and at runtime. This gives application developers the possibility to protect their applications, in particular the application's interfaces, from being misused by unauthorized or malicious applications. For instance, a developer can specify which permissions the opponent applications must be assigned in order to access the application's interface. Note that this goes beyond the standard Android permission model where developers can only attach a single permission to an interface. Although SAINT offers a flexible and fine-grained access control mechanism for Android applications, it requires developers to accurately define and deploy SAINT policies themselves.

Aquifer [103] is a modified Android version which allows application developers and/or users to define UI workflow policies for data they process. A UI workflow policy defines allowed and necessary steps a user has to perform before an action is triggered. For example, an email client might enforce that the user may only use a defined office suite to modify documents, and that the email client is the only application which may send this document to other recipients. Aquifer consists of a Linux Security Module which mediates kernel-level access control (e.g., access to the document file) and middleware extensions to track and control UI interaction. A limitation

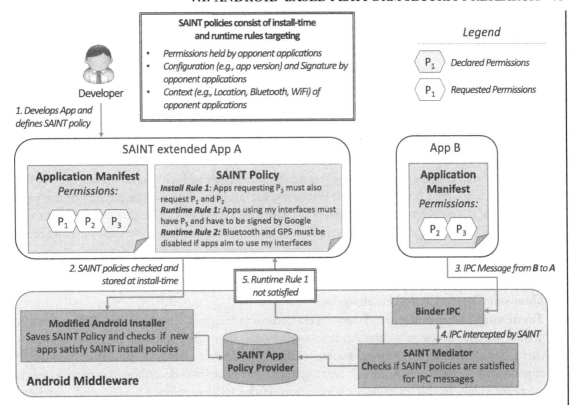

Figure 7.10: Abstract architecture and workflow of SAINT.

of Aquifer is that it requires application developers to adhere to their system model, meaning to define correct information flow policies, a cumbersome process and error-prone process.

Inline Reference Monitors (IRMs) enable fine-grained access control by extending applications with a reference monitor [44]. In the case of Android, IRM enable additional access control mechanisms without requiring a modification to the Android operating system. The key insight of IRMs is to incorporate policy enforcement points and code into existing applications. At runtime, the application flow is redirected to the policy enforcement code which validate whether an API call adheres to a pre-defined policy.

One example for an IRM is **AppGuard**, a tool which modifies the Dalvik bytecode of applications and redirects calls to security- and privacy-critical APIs to the policy enforcement code [14]. Similarly, **Dr. Android** and **Mr. Hide** redirect the execution to a filtering service [81]. Another IRM solution for Android is **Aurasium** which is based on injecting a native library into an application [116]. This library executes at application load-time and instruments the Global

Offset Table (GOT) of the application to redirect the control-flow of an application to policy enforcement code.

Although IRM solutions do not require a jailbreak of the device, they suffer from several deficiencies. First, the policy enforcement code is residing inside the same memory area as the application itself. Hence, a malicious application that is aware of an IRM can directly change and revert the IRM code by means of native code or Java reflection. Second, IRM solutions still require changes to application packages and hence the original developer certificate is no longer valid.

CRePE (Context-Related Policy Enforcement for Android) enables the enforcement of context-related policies [30]. Hence, users may define policies which enable/disable certain functionalities (e.g., read SMS, bluetooth discovery, GPS) depending on the context of the phone (e.g., location, temperature, noise, user, etc.). Moreover, contexts can be also defined by a trusted third-party facilitating, for instance, employers to enforce a company-wide policy for all employees owning Android smartphones.

Mandatory Access Control Frameworks

TrustDroid [23] uses the mandatory access control paradigm to establish isolated business and private security domains on the Android operating system. Applications are classified into security domains using an optional Reference Integrity Metric (RIM) certificate embedded into applications. A RIM certificate is a cryptographic certificate that describes an expected integrity reference value, in this case for an application. If the RIM certificate is valid and matches an application, the corresponding app it is assigned to the business domain. TrustDroid uses synchronized middleware- and kernel-level policy enforcement points to mediate access on resources. New resources are tagged based on the security domain of the application which created it. On the kernel-level, Trustdroid uses a combination of the Tomoyo [71] MAC module and the Net-filter packet filter to control access to kernel-level resources, such as files created by applications and TCP/IP networks. On the middleware-level, system components (e.g., the ContactsProvider which manages contacts and the Activitymanager which manages application interaction) enforce access to resources depending on the security domain of the calling application (e.g., a contact created by a business application is not accessible by a private application). A limitation of Trust-Droid is that it is not generic, i.e., it uses a static use-case specific policy to separate business and private resources and applications.

FlaskDroid is a flexible access control architecture which combines kernel- and middleware-layer policy enforcement into a synchronized framework [24]. It is based on type enforcement and applies the concept of Userspace Object Managers (USOMs) to the middleware layer. USOMs provide fine-grained access control on the types of data they manage, e.g., sensor data, contacts information, and Binder IPC messages. Combined with kernel-level enforcement (cf. Figure 7.11) FlaskDroid's design supports multiple stakeholders (e.g., administrators, users, app developers), context-aware access control policies (e.g., blocking access to sensors while the device is used in a privacy-sensitive context) and allows for policy-driven instantiation of related work, such as SAINT and XManDroid.

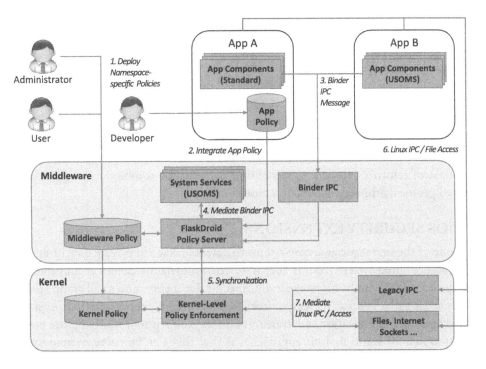

·**Figure 7.11:** Architecture and example workflow of FlaskDroid.

While, in general, type enforcement can provide very fine-grained access control, the required policies tend to be complex. On mobile devices, however, type enforcement policies lean towards much less complexity than on desktop and server systems, mainly due to the convergence of functionality into system components and clearly defined interfaces. To further facilitate policy design FlaskDroid supports a learning mode in which policy rules are derived from user interaction, and provides intuitive graphical user interfaces to configure policies for specific use cases, such as fine-grained access control to contacts data. An open-source implementation of FlaskDroid for the Android operating system based on Security Enhanced Android (SE Android) is available at http://www.flaskdroid.org.

7.2 PLATFORM SECURITY RESEARCH ON IOS

For the sake of completeness, we briefly elaborate on recently proposed security extensions for the closed-source iOS.

7.2.1   LIMITS OF APPLE'S APPLICATION VETTING PROCESS

Several researchers have recently investigated the effectiveness of Apple's application review (vetting) process, and showed how one can inject malware without being detected by the vetting process. Han et al. demonstrate that it is possible to use the (prohibited) private frameworks [70]. The main idea is to dynamically load a private framework at runtime, where the code that performs the dynamic load is obfuscated and can be hardly recognized by static analysis tools. Moreover, the authors also show how to invoke unauthorized private API calls.

Wang et al. use a slightly different approach to hide malicious actions [140]. Specifically, they embed vulnerabilities (e.g., a buffer overflow) into an application. Hence, the application does not contain malicious code at the time it is submitted to the App Store. However, once installed on the user's device, the attacker sends a payload that exploits the vulnerability and uses the principle of return-oriented programming to afterwards combine existing code pieces (i.e., gadgets) to perform arbitrary malicious actions.

7.2.2   IOS SECURITY EXTENSIONS

PiOS is one of the first static analysis systems to detect leakage of private data by applications for Apple's iOS operating system [35]. It does not perform dynamic checks at runtime, but analyzes the binary code of iOS applications statically. Specifically, it generates a call graph from the binary and looks at all paths from a "privacy source" to a "sink" and checks whether private data (such as address book or GPS location) are transmitted to a sink without notifying the user. However, a known problem of static analysis approaches is that they can be circumvented by obfuscation techniques and are limited in their effectiveness because they do not cover the runtime behavior of an application.

MoCFI is a runtime enforcement system that mitigates runtime attacks such as return-oriented programming [33]. It generates the control-flow graph (CFG) of an application based on PiOS in a static analysis phase. At load-time of an application, MoCFI rewrites the binary in memory to incorporate control-flow checks at each indirect branch instruction. When the application is executing the control-flow checks validate whether the program's control-flow is according to the pre-determined CFG. This ensures the property of control-flow integrity (CFI). On the downside, MoCFI introduces performance overhead when applied to computationally-intensive apps, and still requires a jailbreak due to Apple's code signing enforcement (see Section 4.3.3) which prohibits any changes to executable code pages.

In a follow-up work, the MoCFI framework has been used to enable fine-grained sandboxing rules for iOS applications in a tool called **PSiOS** [142]. In particular, PSiOS extends MoCFI by also validating API and system calls to a pre-defined and app-specific policy. This tackles the problem that all third-party iOS applications share one single sandboxing profile. For instance, this can be used to prevent the leakage of private data at runtime. Nevertheless, PSiOS inherits the jailbreak and performance problem of MoCFI.

7.3 DISCUSSION

While a majority of the research community recently has been focusing on Android and iOS, many of the above described works also apply to other mobile operating systems. The concrete implementation and design might vary depending on platform, but the overall idea and principles remain the same.

The number of privilege escalation attacks with the goal of escaping from a sandbox environment or getting additional permissions via an abuse of a legitimate application is constantly rising for many mobile operating systems [95]. This makes the deployment of systems similar to QUIRE or XManDroid very valuable to other platforms. With the regards to the kernel-based privileged escalations the introduction of the mandatory access control frameworks, like SEAndroid or Smack [126] in Tizen, together with the various kernel hardening mechanisms is also a continuous trend in the mobile operating system security design.

Type-based Access control frameworks operating on all layers of the operating system, such as SEAndroid and FlaskDroid, have demonstrated that the adoption of type enforcement in the context of smart mobile devices is generally feasible. However, type enforcement requires considerable effort for policy engineering and labelling of subjects and objects. Other approaches might be more feasible for adoption on mobile devices. Furthermore, it has been shown that policy conflict resolution is a difficult problem which is a particular problem considering multiple stakeholders who want to protect their individual interests.

One approach to provide a more general system-centric access control architecture is to use a *modular* framework. Similar to the Linux Security Modules kernel-level access control framework [144], in such an architecture generic enforcement hooks are placed into all security-critical kernel- and middleware software components. Individual use-case and stakeholder specific security modules can serve as policy decision points for access control decisions within their respective domains. By abstracting the actual access control decision logic, such an architecture allows the individual modules to implement different security models within their respective domains.

In context of multiple stakeholders, for example in the BYOD context, virtualization is a valid approach to isolate security domains. Hardware virtualization support on smart mobile devices is currently becoming available and it remains to be seen if virtualization is suitable for daily use considering open security and usability challenges. On the one hand, frequent manual domain switches are tedious and time-consuming for users, a challenging problem which needs to be addressed in future work. On the other hand, virtualization only provides coarse-grained domain isolation by containing potentially malicious activities inside isolated security domains. Fine-grained access control on sensitive data thus requires an efficient combination of virtualization and system-centric access control frameworks inside the separate security domains.

The enhancements to an application installer similar to Kirin or Apex can add a benefit to the platforms that only rely on a user to make security decisions, because they can provide an additional information about potential collisions or warn about sensitive permissions being asked. Similarly, systems like TaintDroid or AppFence can warn user about privacy information leakage that can happen on any platform. Preserving legacy compliance, meaning preventing applications from crashing when they are denied access to resources, is a challenging problem which needs to be considered in this context.

It can be beneficial to integrate to application stores various static analysis tools like Com-Droid, Stowaway, or PiOS in order to provide a better application filtering and notify developers if their applications are overprivileged or contain potential vulnerabilities. Moreover, such checks can be already done by a platform SDK in order to guide developers to a better application design.

Context-related policy enforcement systems like CRePE can bring an additional benefit to any mobile platform since it allows having finer-grained policies that can be conveniently configured using gathered contextual information. Furthermore, they have the potential to further simplify the secure configuration of smart devices for end users via semi-automatic detection of dangerous contexts and automatic configuration of corresponding access control rules. While the above systems can bring additional value to the security of mobile operating systems, their deployment cost, performance implications, and in some cases, more complex usage patterns should be carefully analyzed beforehand.

Despite the extensive and widespread deployment of mobile platform security architectures, as with any non-trivial systems, it is inevitable that there will be design, implementation, or configuration errors in them. Attackers will develop malware that exploit these errors. Over the past few years, there have been several reports of alarming increases in the number of malware samples discovered, especially for the Android platform. However, there is very little information on the actual rate of infection among mobile devices.

Recent work by independent researchers have tried to address the question of estimating malware infection rate in mobile devices. Lever et al. [88] used the indirect method of inferring infection by analyzing domain name resolution queries. They concluded that the infection rate in the United States is less than 0.0009%. Truong et al. [74] used data collected directly from over 50,000 Android devices and arrived at a rough estimate of 0.3%.

CHAPTER 8

Conclusions

This book has presented an overview of mobile platform security. We have described a generic model for mobile platform security architectures. The model illustrates commonly used security mechanisms and components in mobile devices, and using this model we have analyzed several mobile platforms. We have explained typical hardware-security techniques and surveyed recent research in the area of mobile platform security. The main conclusions of this book are the following.

- The security architectures in all noteworthy mobile platforms are based on a similar model. The main deployed security techniques are permission-based access control, code signing, and application isolation.

- Most of the security mechanisms used in the currently popular smartphone platforms are not new, but adapted from previous mobile platforms. The current state of smartphone platform security is a result of a long evolution in mobile phone security.

- Unlike PC platforms, many mobile devices have incorporated hardware-based security techniques for almost a decade. The adoption of hardware security in the mobile domain has been steered by requirements from the regulators and the operators.

- Mobile platform security is currently an active research area. Privilege-escalation attacks, detection of malicious applications, and application hardening are examples of research topics that have gathered considerable attention in the research community. Despite many proposed solutions, unsolved problems remain.

For the near future, we see the following major trends in mobile platform security. Public hardware-security APIs will pave the way for more widespread adoption of third-party hardware-assisted security services in mobile devices. At the moment, the Global Platform industry alliance is leading this development. Hopefully, the mobile industry will adopt an open provisioning model that would allow free deployment of hardware-security services in mobile devices.

Many mobile platforms support application development using web development techniques (JavaScript, HTML 5 and CSS). Windows Phone 8, iOS, and BlackBerry 10 are examples of currently widely used mobile platforms that support web applications, while Tizen, WebOS, and Firefox OS are examples of emerging mobile platforms in which all application development is based on web programming model. In these platforms, introduction of new executable code (web or native) is controlled by an installer component that assigns permissions for the application execution. In future mobile platforms, mobile web applications may be able to dynamically load executable code from an online service. Such application model would allow faster deployment of new features in mobile online services. At the same time, possibility to execute downloaded code would change the notion of a mobile application, and have effects on the established mobile platform security model. If the executable code of a mobile application may change at runtime, installation-time permission assignment cannot be used to control application execution. Adoption of such dynamic web development model would imply that certain aspects of the existing mobile platform security architectures would have to be redesigned.

The distinction between mobile platforms and PC platforms is constantly blurring. To control the execution of applications from malicious developers, the PC platform providers have started to adopt security mechanisms from mobile platforms. Both in the Windows 8 and recent Mac OS X platforms, marketplaces are used to distribute applications and marketplace operators assign permissions to applications and sign them. As more features are included into mobile devices, smartphone platforms approach PC platforms in functionality. New mobile device form factors increasingly diminish the traditional differences between mobile devices and PCs. The security mechanisms used in mobile devices and PCs are likely to merge. We hope that the platform security model defined in this book will help in the development of such future platforms.

Bibliography

[1] European telecommunications standards institute. `http://www.etsi.org`. 2

[2] Federal communications commission. `http://www.fcc.gov`. 2

[3] Mer project. `http://merproject.org`. 19

[4] Tizen. `https://www.tizen.org/`. 26

[5] Dev-team blog, 2013. `http://blog.iphone-dev.org/`. 42

[6] 3LM. Three laws of mobility. `http://www.3lm.com/`. 59

[7] A. One. Smashing the stack for fun and profit. *Phrack Magazine*, 1996. 37

[8] Apple Inc. Enabling app sandbox. `http://developer.apple.com/library/ios/#documentation/Miscellaneous/Reference/EntitlementKeyReference/Chapters/EnablingAppSandbox.html#//apple_ref/doc/uid/TP40011195-CH4-SW1`, 2012. 25

[9] Apple Inc. iOS security. `http://images.apple.com/ipad/business/docs/iOS_Security_May12.pdf`, 2012. 25, 39

[10] Apple Inc. iOS SDK release notes for iOS 6. `http://developer.apple.com/library/ios/#releasenotes/General/RN-iOSSDK-6_0/index.html`, 2013. 24

[11] W.A. Arbaugh, D.J. Farber, and J.M. Smith. A secure and reliable bootstrap architecture. In *IEEE Symposium on Security and Privacy*, 1997. DOI: 10.1109/SECPRI.1997.601317. 17

[12] ARM. TrustZone-enabled processor. `http://www.arm.com/products/processors/technologies/trustzone.php`. 16, 50

[13] ARM. Building a secure system using TrustZone™ technology, 2009. `http://infocenter.arm.com/help/topic/com.arm.doc.prd29-genc-009492c/PRD29-GENC-009492C_trustzone_security_whitepaper.pdf`. 16, 50

[14] M. Backes, S. Gerling, C. Hammer, M. Maffei, and P. von Styp-Rekowsky. App-Guard - enforcing user requirements on Android apps. In *19th International Conference on Tools and Algorithms for the Construction and Analysis of Systems*, TACAS'13, 2013. DOI: 10.1007/978-3-642-36742-7_39. 75

[15] S. Balfe, E. Gallery, C.J. Mitchell, and K.G. Paterson. Challenges for trusted computing. *IEEE Security and Privacy*, 2008. DOI: 10.1109/MSP.2008.138. 2

[16] K. Barr, P. Bungale, S. Deasy, V. Gyuris, P. Hung, C. Newell, H. Tuch, and B. Zoppis. The VMware mobile virtualization platform: is that a hypervisor in your pocket? *SIGOPS Operating Systems Review*, 2010. DOI: 10.1145/1899928.1899945. 59

[17] D. Barrera, W. Enck, and P.C. van Oorschot. Meteor: Seeding a security-enhancing infrastructure for multi-market application ecosystems. In *Mobile Security Technologies Workshop*, MoST'12, 2012. 74

[18] M. Becher, F.C. Freiling, J. Hoffmann, T. Holz, S. Uellenbeck, and C. Wolf. Mobile security catching up? Revealing the nuts and bolts of the security of mobile devices. In *IEEE Symposium on Security and Privacy*, SP'11, 2011. DOI: 10.1109/SP.2011.29. 4

[19] K. Beckert. Android malware barometer shows that a storm is brewing. http://blog.gdatasoftware.com/blog/article/android-malware-barometer-shows-that-a-storm-is-brewing.html, 2013. 63

[20] F. Bellard. QEMU, a fast and portable dynamic translator. In *USENIX Annual Technical Conference*, ATEC'05, 2005. 73

[21] Mathias Bonn. Tutorial: How to Hack your Symbian Device. http://symbian-developers.net/tutorial-how-to-hack-your-symbian-device/. 44

[22] Tim Brookes. Hack Your Symbian Mobile Phone With HelloOx2. http://www.makeuseof.com/tag/hack-symbian-phone-helloox2/. 44

[23] S. Bugiel, L. Davi, A. Dmitrienko, S. Heuser, A.-R. Sadeghi, and B. Shastry. Practical and lightweight domain isolation on Android. In *1st ACM workshop on Security and privacy in smartphones and mobile devices*, SPSM'11, 2011. DOI: 10.1145/2046614.2046624. 76

[24] S. Bugiel, S. Heuser, and A.-R. Sadeghi. Flexible and fine-grained mandatory access control on Android for diverse security and privacy policies. In *22nd USENIX Security Symposium*, 2013. 76

[25] Desktop bus project page. http://www.freedesktop.org/wiki/Software/dbus, 2010. 26

[26] Cellrox Ltd. Cellrox. http://www.cellrox.com/. 59

[27] Chainfire. CF-Auto-Root. http://autoroot.chainfire.eu/. 43

[28] Chainfire. SuperSU - Android Apps on Google Play. https://play.google.com/store/apps/details?id=eu.chainfire.supersu. 43

[29] E. Chin, A.P. Felt, K. Greenwood, and D. Wagner. Analyzing inter-application communication in Android. In *9th International Conference on Mobile Systems, Applications, and Services*, MobiSys'11, 2011. DOI: 10.1145/1999995.2000018. 72

[30] M. Conti, V.T.N. Nguyen, and B. Crispo. CRePE: Context-related policy enforcement for Android. In *13th Information Security Conference*, ISC'10, 2010. DOI: 10.1007/978-3-642-18178-8_29. 76

[31] C. Cowan, C. Pu, D. Maier, H. Hintony, J. Walpole, P. Bakke, S. Beattie, A. Grier, P. Wagle, and Q. Zhang. StackGuard: Automatic adaptive detection and prevention of buffer-overflow attacks. In *USENIX Security Symposium*, 1998. 37

[32] D. A. Dai Zovi. Apple iOS security evaluation. In *Black Hat USA*, 2011. 24, 37

[33] L. Davi, A. Dmitrienko, M. Egele, T. Fischer, T. Holz, R. Hund, S. Nurnberger, and A.-R. Sadeghi. MoCFI: A framework to mitigate control-flow attacks on smartphones. In *19th Annual Network and Distributed System Security Symposium*, NDSS'12, 2012. 78

[34] M. Dietz, S. Shekhar, Y. Pisetsky, A. Shu, and D.S. Wallach. QUIRE: Lightweight provenance for smartphone operating systems. In *20th USENIX Security Symposium*, 2011. 64, 70

[35] M. Egele, C. Kruegel, E. Kirda, and G. Vigna. PiOS: detecting privacy leaks in iOS applications. In *18th Annual Network and Distributed System Security Symposium*, NDSS'11, 2011. 78

[36] J.-E. Ekberg. *Securing Software Architectures for Trusted Processor Environments*. PhD thesis, Aalto University, 2013. 51

[37] J.-E. Ekberg, K. Kostiainen, and N. Asokan. The untapped potential of trusted execution environments on mobile devices. *IEEE Security and Privacy magazine*. To appear. DOI: 10.1007/978-3-642-39884-1_24. 53

[38] N. Elenkov. Using app encryption in Jelly Bean, 2012. `http://nelenkov.blogspot.ch/2012/07/jelly-bean-hardware-backed-credential.html`. 41

[39] W. Enck. Defending users against smartphone apps: Techniques and future directions. In *International Conference on Information Systems Security*, ICISS, 2011. DOI: 10.1007/978-3-642-25560-1_3. 4

[40] W. Enck, P. Gilbert, B.-G. Chun, L.P. Cox, J. Jung, P. McDaniel, and A.N. Sheth. TaintDroid: an information-flow tracking system for realtime privacy monitoring on smartphones. In *9th USENIX Conference on Operating Systems Design and Implementation*, OSDI'10, 2010. 68

[41] W. Enck, D. Octeau, P. McDaniel, and S. Chaudhuri. A study of Android application security. In *USENIX Security Symposium*, 2011. 4, 72

[42] W. Enck, M. Ongtang, and P. McDaniel. Mitigating Android software misuse before it happens. Technical Report NAS-TR-0094-2008, Pennsylvania State University, 2008. 68

[43] W. Enck, M. Ongtang, and P. McDaniel. On lightweight mobile phone application certification. In *16th ACM Conference on Computer and Communications Security*, CCS'09, 2009. DOI: 10.1145/1653662.1653691. 62, 68

[44] U. Erlingsson. *The inlined reference monitor approach to security policy enforcement.* PhD thesis, Cornell University, Ithaca, NY, USA, 2004. AAI3114521. 75

[45] ETSI. *ETSI GSM 02.09 Security Aspects.* European Telecommunication Standards Institute, 1993. Version 3.1.0; http://www.3gpp.org/ftp/Specs/html-info/0209.htm. 2

[46] ETSI. *ETSI GSM 02.09 Security Aspects.* European Telecommunication Standards Institute, 2001. Version 8.0.1, Release 99; http://www.3gpp.org/ftp/Specs/html-info/0209.htm. 3

[47] A.P. Felt, E. Chin, S. Hanna, D. Song, and D. Wagner. Android permissions demystified. In *18th ACM Conference on Computer and Communications Security*, CCS'11, 2011. DOI: 10.1145/2046707.2046779. 72

[48] A.P. Felt, M. Finifter, E. Chin, S. Hanna, and D. Wagner. A survey of mobile malware in the wild. In *ACM Workshop on Security and Privacy in Smartphones and Mobile Devices*, SPSM'11, 2011. DOI: 10.1145/2046614.2046618. 16

[49] A.P. Felt, H. Wang, A. Moshchuk, S. Hanna, and E. Chin. Permission re-delegation: Attacks and defenses. In *20th USENIX Security Symposium*, 2011. 65

[50] E. Fragkaki, L. Bauer, L. Jia, and D. Swasey. Modeling and enhancing Android's permission system. In *17th European Symposium on Research in Computer Security*, ESORICS'12, 2012. DOI: 10.1007/978-3-642-33167-1_1. 66

[51] Fraunhofer AISEC. Trust|me.
http://www.aisec.fraunhofer.de/de/kompetenzen/trustme.html. 59

[52] Fraunhofer SIT. BizzTrust. http://www.bizztrust.de. 59

[53] Gartner, Inc. Gartner says worldwide PC, tablet and mobile phone shipments to grow 5.9 percent in 2013 as anytime-anywhere-computing drives buyer behavior. http://www.gartner.com/newsroom/id/2525515. 22

[54] Gartner, Inc. Magic quadrant for mobile device management software. `http://www.citrix.com/news/awards-and-reviews/may-2013/gartner-mobile-device-management-magic-quadrant.html`. 59

[55] Giesecke and Devrient. Mobicore: Giesecke and Devrient's secure OS for ARM Trust-Zone technology, 2011. `http://www.gi-de.com`. 51

[56] Gitorious. MSSF project source code. `http://meego.gitorious.org/meego-platform-security`, 2010. 26

[57] Global Platform. TEE client API specification v1.0, 2010. `http://www.globalplatform.org`. 52

[58] Global Platform. TEE internal API specification v1.0, 2011. `http://www.globalplatform.org`. 52

[59] Global Platform. TEE system architecture v1.0, 2011. `http://www.globalplatform.org`. 51, 52

[60] Global Platform. A new model: The consumer-centric model and how it applies to the mobile ecosystem, 2012. `http://www.globalplatform.org/documents/Consumer_Centric_Model_White_PaperMar2012.pdf`. 52

[61] GlobalPlatform. GlobalPlatform's GPD/STIP solution for mobile security, 2007. GlobalPlatform white paper. `http://www.globalplatform.org/uploads/STIP_WhitePaper.pdf`. 51

[62] Good Technology. Good Technology. `http://www1.good.com`. DOI: 10.1017/S0007087402244611. 58

[63] Google. Android 4.3 APIs | Android developers. `http://developer.android.com/about/versions/android-4.3.html`. 24

[64] Google. Android permissions. `https://developer.android.com/guide/topics/manifest/permission-element.html#plevel`. 33

[65] Google. Security enhancements in Android 4.3. `http://source.android.com/devices/tech/security/enhancements43.html`. 39

[66] Google. Security enhancements in Android 4.4. `http://developer.android.com/about/versions/kitkat.html#44-security`. 24

[67] M.C. Grace, W. Zhou, X. Jiang, and A.-R. Sadeghi. Unsafe exposure analysis of mobile in-app advertisements. In *5th ACM Conference on Security and Privacy in Wireless and Mobile Networks*, WiSec'12, 2012. DOI: 10.1145/2185448.2185464. 63

[68] H. Shacham. The geometry of innocent flesh on the bone: Return-into-libc without function calls (on the x86). In *ACM Conference on Computer and Communications Security (CCS)*, 2007. DOI: 10.1145/1315245.1315313. 37

[69] hackcracks.com. Windows Phone 8 Jailbreak. `http://hackcracks.com/jailbreaks/windows-phone-8-jailbreak.html`. 44

[70] J. Han, S.M. Kywe, Q. Yan, F. Bao, R. Deng, D. Gao, Y. Li, and J. Zhou. Launching generic attacks on iOS with approved third-party applications. In *International Conference on Applied Cryptography and Network Security*, ACNS'13, 2013. DOI: 10.1007/978-3-642-38980-1_17. 78

[71] T. Harada, T. Horie, and K. Tanaka. Task oriented management obviates your onus on Linux. In *Linux Conference*, 2004. 68, 76

[72] N. Hardy. The confused deputy: (or why capabilities might have been invented). *SIGOPS Operating Systems Review*, 1988. DOI: 10.1145/54289.871709. 62

[73] C. Heath. *Symbian OS Platform Security*. Wiley, 2006. 22

[74] Petteri Nurmi, Adam J. Oliner, Sasu Tarkoma, N. Asokan, Hien Thi Thu Truong, Eemil Lagerspetz, and Sourav Bhattacharya. The company you keep: Mobile malware infection rates and inexpensive risk indicators. Technical Report arXiv:1312.3245, arXiv.org, Dec 2013. `http://arxiv.org/abs/1312.3245`. 80

[75] P. Hornyack, S. Han, J. Jung, S. Schechter, and D. Wetherall. These aren't the droids you're looking for: Retrofitting Android to protect data from imperious applications. In *18th ACM conference on Computer and Communications Security*, CCS'11, 2011. DOI: 10.1145/2046707.2046780. 69

[76] D. Hurlbut. Fuzzy hashing for digital forensic investigators. Technical Report TR-syssec-11-01, Access Data Inc., May 2011. 73

[77] Enterproid Inc. The Divide platform enables BYOD mobility - Divide. `http://www.divide.com/`. 58

[78] V. Iozzo and C. Miller. Fun and games with Mac OS X and iPhone payloads. In *Black Hat Europe*, 2009. 37

[79] V. Iozzo and R. Weinmann. PWN2OWN contest. `http://blog.zynamics.com/2010/03/24/ralf-philipp-weinmann-vincenzo-iozzo-own-the-iphone-at-pwn2own/`, 2010. 37

[80] jackburton. [HOWTO] Compiling new kernels on Harmattan device. `http://talk.maemo.org/showthread.php?t=89507`. 44

[81] J. Jeon, K.K. Micinski, J.A. Vaughan, A. Fogel, N. Reddy, J.S. Foster, and T. Millstein. Dr. Android and Mr. Hide: Fine-grained permissions in Android applications. In *2nd ACM Workshop on Security and Privacy in Smartphones and Mobile Devices*, SPSM'12, 2012. DOI: 10.1145/2381934.2381938. 75

[82] Jolla. Sailfish OS. `https://sailfishos.org/`. 26

[83] D. Kasatkin. Mobile simplified security framework. In *12th Linux Symposium*, 2010. 19, 26

[84] MJ Keith. Android 2.0-2.1 reverse shell exploit, 2010. `http://www.exploit-db.com/exploits/15423/`. 37

[85] K. Kostiainen and N. Asokan. Credential life cycle management in open credential platforms (short paper). In *ACM Workshop on Scalable Trusted Computing*, STC'11, 2011. DOI: 10.1145/2046582.2046595. 53

[86] K. Kostiainen, J.-E. Ekberg, N. Asokan, and A. Rantala. On-board credentials with open provisioning. In *ACM Symposium on Information, Computer & Communications Security*, ASIACCS'09, 2009. DOI: 10.1145/1533057.1533074. 51

[87] M. Lange, S. Liebergeld, A. Lackorzynski, A. Warg, and M. Peter. L4Android: a generic operating system framework for secure smartphones. In *1st ACM Workshop on Security and Privacy in Smartphones and Mobile Devices*, SPSM'11, 2011. DOI: 10.1145/2046614.2046623. 68

[88] Charles Lever, Manos Antonakakis, Bradley Reaves, Patrick Traynor, and Wenke Lee. The core of the matter: Analyzing malicious traffic in cellular carriers. In *NDSS*. The Internet Society, 2013. 80

[89] S. Litchfield. Defining the smartphone. Online article at AllAboutSymbian.com, 2010. `http://www.allaboutsymbian.com/features/item/Defining_the_Smartphone.php`. 1

[90] P. Loscocco and S. Smalley. Integrating flexible support for security policies into the Linux operating system. In *USENIX Annual Technical Conference, FREENIX Track*, ATEC'01, 2001. 1

[91] L. Lu, Z. Li, Z. Wu, W. Lee, and G. Jiang. CHEX: Statically vetting Android apps for component hijacking vulnerabilities. In *19th ACM Conference on Computer and Communications Security*, CCS'12, 2012. DOI: 10.1145/2382196.2382223. 72

[92] S. Khan M. Nauman and X. Zhang. Apex: Extending Android permission model and enforcement with user-defined runtime constraints. In *5th ACM Symposium*

on Information, Computer and Communications Security, ASIACCS'10, 2010. DOI: 10.1145/1755688.1755732. 68

[93] Aemon Malone. Hackers uncover new pdf exploit for ios jailbreak. http://www.digitaltrends.com/mobile/hackers-uncover-new-pdf-exploit-for-ios-jailbreak/, 2011. 43

[94] C. Marforio, H. Ritzdorf, A. Francillon, and S. Capkun. Analysis of the communication between colluding applications on modern smartphones. In *28th Annual Computer Security Applications Conference*, ACSAC'12, 2012. 62

[95] McAfee. Mobile malware growth continuing in 2013. http://www.mcafee.com/us/security-awareness/articles/mobile-malware-growth-continuing-2013.aspx, 2013. 79

[96] MeeGo. Mobile simplified security framework overview. http://conference2010.meego.com/session/mobile-simplified-security-framework-overview, 2010. 26

[97] Microsoft. How to register your phone for development. http://msdn.microsoft.com/en-us/library/windowsphone/develop/ff769508%28v=vs.105%29.aspx. 44

[98] Microsoft. Windows Phone 7.5 enterprise security and policy management, 2011. http://www.microsoft.com/download/en/details.aspx?id=27743. 27

[99] Microsoft TechCenter. Securing the Windows 8 boot process, 2013. http://technet.microsoft.com/en-us/windows/dn168167.aspx. 2

[100] Sun Microsystems. Mobile information device profile for Java 2 Micro Edition, v2.1. http://www.oracle.com/technetwork/java/index-jsp-138820.html, 2006. 1, 3, 19, 32

[101] MobileIron Inc. MobileIron | The Platform for Mobile IT. http://www.mobileiron.com. 59

[102] C. Mulliner and C. Miller. Injecting SMS messages into smart phones for security analysis. In *USENIX Workshop on Offensive Technologies*, WOOT, 2009. 37

[103] A. Nadkarni and W. Enck. Preventing accidental data disclosure in modern operating systems. In *2013 ACM Conference on Computer and Communications Security*, CCS. ACM, 2013. DOI: 10.1145/2508859.2516677. 74

[104] Nergal. The advanced return-into-lib(c) exploits: PaX case study. *Phrack Magazine*, 2001. 37

[105] Nokia.   MeeGo 1.2 Harmattan Developer Documentation.   `http://harmattan-dev.nokia.com/docs/library/html/guide/html/Developer_Library_Developing_for_Harmattan_Activating_developer_mode.html`. 44

[106] NSA. SELinux Wiki: SEAndroid. `http://selinuxproject.org/page/SEAndroid`, 2012. 24, 67

[107] J. Oberheide.   Exploit mitigations in Android Jelly Bean 4.1.   `https://blog.duosecurity.com/2012/07/exploit-mitigations-in-android-jelly-bean-4-1/`, 2012. 37

[108] T. Oi. Windows Phone 7 internals and explotability. In *BlackHat USA*, 2012. 38

[109] M. Ongtang, K. Butler, and P. McDaniel. Porscha: Policy oriented secure content handling in Android. In *26th Annual Computer Security Applications Conference*, ACSAC'10, 2010. DOI: 10.1145/1920261.1920295. 70

[110] M. Ongtang, S. McLaughlin, W. Enck, and P. McDaniel. Semantically rich application-centric security in Android. In *25th Annual Computer Security Applications Conference*, ACSAC'09, 2009. DOI: 10.1109/ACSAC.2009.39. 74

[111] Oracle. JSR 177: Security and trust services API for J2ME, 2007. `http://jcp.org/en/jsr/detail?id=177`. 21, 38, 51

[112] Oracle. Java technology. `http://www.java.com/en/about/`, 2010. 1

[113] P. Pearce, A.P. Felt, G. Nunez, and D. Wagner. AdDroid: Privilege separation for applications and advertisers in Android. In *7th ACM Symposium on Information, Computer and Communications Security*, ASIACCS'12, 2012. DOI: 10.1145/2414456.2414498. 71

[114] G. Portokalidis, P. Homburg, K. Anagnostakis, and H. Bos. Paranoid Android: Versatile protection for smartphones. In *26th Annual Computer Security Applications Conference*, ACSAC'10, 2010. DOI: 10.1145/1920261.1920313. 73

[115] B. Prince.   Security expert evades Apple's mobile security measures via iOS vulnerability.   `http://s1.securityweek.com/apple-security-expert-evades-apples-mobile-security-measures-ios-vulnerability`, 2011. 37

[116] H. Saïdi R. Xu and R. Anderson. Aurasium: Practical policy enforcement for Android applications. In *21st USENIX Security Symposium*, 2012. 75

[117] E. Reshetova.   Mobile simplified security framework overview.   `http://userweb.kernel.org/~jmorris/lss2010_slides/reshetova_LinuxCon_overview_v_final.pdf`, 2010. 40

[118] F. Roesner and T. Kohno. Securing embedded user interfaces: Android and beyond. In *22nd USENIX Conference on Security*. USENIX Association, 2013. 71

[119] F. Roesner, T. Kohno, A. Moshchuk, B. Parno, H.J. Wang, and C. Cowan. User-driven access control: Rethinking permission granting in modern operating systems. In *2012 IEEE Symposium on Security and Privacy*, SP '12, 2012. DOI: 10.1109/SP.2012.24. 72

[120] S. Bugiel, L. Davi, A. Dmitrienko, T. Fischer, A.-R. Sadeghi and B. Shastry. Towards taming privilege-escalation attacks on Android. In *19th Annual Network & Distributed System Security Symposium*, NDSS'12, 2012. 66, 68

[121] R. Sailer, X. Zhang, T. Jaeger, and L. van Doorn. Design and implementation of a TCG-based integrity measurement architecture. In *13th USENIX Security Symposium*, 2004. 27, 39, 41

[122] J. Sales. *Symbian OS internals*. Wiley, 2005. 22

[123] J. Saltzer and M. Shcroeder. The protection of information in computer systems. *Communications of the ACM*, July 1974. 21

[124] Samsung. SAFE – Samsung for enterprise – Galaxy at work. `www.samsung.com/us/safe`. 59

[125] Samsung. Samsung KNOX-Solutions-Security. `http://www.samsung.com/global/business/mobile/solution/security/samsung-knox`. 59

[126] C. Schaufler. Smack in embedded computing. In *10th Linux Symposium*, 2008. 27, 79

[127] R. Schlegel, K. Zhang, X. Zhou, M. Intwala, A. Kapadia, and X.F. Wang. Soundcomber: a stealthy and context-aware sound Trojan for smartphones. In *18th Annual Network and Distributed System Security Symposium*, NDSS'11, 2011. 62, 66

[128] F.J. Serna. The info leak era on software exploitation. In *Black Hat USA*, 2012. 37

[129] S. Shekhar, M. Dietz, and D.S. Wallach. AdSplit: Separating smartphone advertising from applications. In *21st USENIX Security Symposium*, 2012. 63, 70

[130] Sidharth. Understanding iOS jailbreaking process, and how it really works. `http://blogote.com/apple/how-ios-jailbreak-works/26651/#ixzz2A1tQDutl`, 2012. 42

[131] S. Smalley and R. Craig. Security Enhanced (SE) Android: Bringing flexible MAC to Android. In *20th Annual Network & Distributed System Security Symposium*, NDSS'13, 2013. 59, 67

[132] SourceForge. An overview of the Linux integrity subsystem. `http://heanet.dl.sourceforge.net/project/linux-ima/linux-ima/Integrity_overview.pdf`, 2010. 27, 39, 41

[133] J. Srage and J. Azema. M-Shield mobile security technology, 2005. TI white paper. `http://focus.ti.com/pdfs/wtbu/ti_mshield_whitepaper.pdf`. 45, 50

[134] H. Sundaresan. OMAP platform security features, 2003. TI white paper. `http://focus.ti.com/pdfs/vf/wireless/platformsecuritywp.pdf`. 45

[135] V. Svajcer. First malware using Android Gingerbreak root exploit. `http://nakedsecurity.sophos.com/2011/08/22/first-malware-using-android-gingerbreak-exploit/`, 2011. 67

[136] T-Systems International GmbH. Homeland Security and Defense ICT: Protecting people and nations. `http://www.t-systems.com/industries/homeland-security-and-defense-ict-protecting-people-and-nations/761542`. 59

[137] Trusted Computing Group. `https://www.trustedcomputinggroup.org/home`. 1

[138] TCG. Trusted Platform Module (TPM) specifications. `https://www.trustedcomputinggroup.org/specs/TPM/`. 1

[139] Tizen. Security/application installation and manifest, August 2012. `https://wiki.tizen.org/wiki/Security/Application_installation_and_Manifest`. 26

[140] T. Wang, K. Lu, L. Lu, S. Chung, and W. Lee. Jekyll on iOS: When benign apps become evil. In *USENIX Security Symposium*, 2013. 78

[141] R. Watson. TrustedBSD: Adding trusted operating system features to FreeBSD. In *USENIX Annual Technical Conference*, ATEC'01, 2001. 24

[142] T. Werthmann, R. Hund, L. Davi, A.-R. Sadeghi, and T. Holz. PSiOS: Bring your own privacy & security to iOS devices. In *8th ACM Symposium on Information, Computer and Communications Security*, ASIACCS'13, 2013. DOI: 10.1145/2484313.2484316. 78

[143] J. Wiens. A tipping point for the trusted platform module? *Information Week Security*, 2008. `http://www.informationweek.com/security/encryption/a-tipping-point-for-the-trusted-platform/208800939`. 2

[144] C. Wright, C. Cowan, S. Smalley, J. Morris, and K.-H. Greg. Linux Security Modules: General Security Support for the Linux Kernel. In *11th USENIX Security Symposium*, 2002. 79

[145] L.K. Yan and H. Yin. DroidScope: Seamlessly reconstructing the OS and Dalvik semantic views for dynamic Android malware analysis. In *21st USENIX Security Symposium*, 2012. 73

[146] W. Zhou, Y. Zhou, M. Grace, X. Jiang, and S. Zou. Fast, scalable detection of "piggy-backed" mobile applications. In *3rd ACM Conference on Data and Application Security and Privacy*, CODASPY'13, 2013. DOI: 10.1145/2435349.2435377. 73, 74

[147] W. Zhou, Y. Zhou, X. Jiang, and P. Ning. Detecting repackaged smartphone applications in third-party Android marketplaces. In *2nd ACM Conference on Data and Application Security and Privacy*, CODASPY'12, 2012. DOI: 10.1145/2133601.2133640. 73

[148] Y. Zhou and X. Jiang. Dissecting android malware: Characterization and evolution. In *IEEE Symposium on Security and Privacy*, SP'12, 2012. DOI: 10.1109/SP.2012.16. 16

[149] Y. Zhou, Z. Wang, W. Zhou, and X. Jiang. Hey, you, get off of my market: Detecting malicious apps in official and alternative Android markets. In *19th Annual Network & Distributed System Security Symposium*, NDSS'12, 2012. 73

[150] Y. Zhou, X. Zhang, X. Jiang, and V.W. Freeh. Taming information-stealing smartphone applications (on Android). In *4th international conference on Trust and trustworthy comput-ing*, TRUST'11, 2011. DOI: 10.1007/978-3-642-21599-5_7. 69

Authors' Biographies

N. ASOKAN

Asokan is a Professor at Aalto University and the University of Helsinki. He joined academia recently after a long spell in industrial research at Nokia Research Center and IBM Research. Asokan holds a doctorate in computer science from the University of Waterloo and is an Associate Editor of *ACM Transactions on Information and System Security (TISSEC)*. He is the Lead Academic Principal Investigator for the Intel Collaborative Research Institute for Secure Computing (ICRI-SC) at the University of Helsinki.

LUCAS DAVI

Lucas is a research assistant at the Intel Collaborative Research Institute for Secure Computing (ICRI-SC) at Technische Universität Darmstadt, Germany. He received his M.Sc. in IT-Security from Ruhr-University Bochum, Germany. His current research focuses on runtime attacks such as return-oriented programming (ROP) for ARM and Intel-based systems. He is working on new attack methods and countermeasures against runtime attacks. His further research areas include mobile operating system security and Trusted Computing.

ALEXANDRA DMITRIENKO

Alexandra is a research assistant at Fraunhofer Institute for Secure Information Technology in Darmstadt (Germany). She obtained her M.Sc. in IT-Security from the Saint-Petersburg State Polytechnical University in Russia. Her achievements in research were honored by the Intel Doctoral Student Honor Award. Her research is mainly focused on security aspects of mobile operating systems and secure mobile applications, in particular, online banking, mobile payments, and ticketing.

STEPHAN HEUSER

Stephan is a research assistant at the Intel Collaborative Research Institute for Secure Computing (ICRI-SC) at Technische Universität Darmstadt, Germany. He received his diploma (M.Sc.) in computer science from Technische Universität Darmstadt, Germany. Before joining ICRI-SC Stephan was employed by Fraunhofer Institute for Secure Information Technology (SIT) in Darmstadt, Germany, where he focused on operating system and application security for mobile devices, network security, and trusted computing. His current research mainly focuses on access control architectures for mobile devices, such as BizzTrust and FlaskDroid security architectures for Android.

KARI KOSTIAINEN

Kari is a postdoctoral researcher at System Security Group of ETH Zurich. His research focus is on security and privacy issues of mobile devices. Before joining ETH, Kari spent several years at Nokia Research Center in Helsinki, and also briefly in Palo Alto. Kari has a doctorate in computer science from Aalto University. In his dissertation, Kari studied mobile platform security mechanisms and developed On-board Credentials platform that is deployed to many Nokia devices. Kari has also contributed to industry standards, including the security architecture of MirrorLink system.

ELENA RESHETOVA

Elena is a Security Architect at the Intel Open Source Technology Center working with various Open Source platform security projects across the whole Linux platform security community. Prior to working for Intel, Elena was employed by Nokia to act as a Security Architect for the Meego platform. Elena is also a postgraduate student at the Aalto University. Her current research area involves exploring various OS virtualization solutions and their applicability for mobile security use cases.

AHMAD-REZA SADEGHI

Ahmad is a full professor of computer science at Technische Universität Darmstadt, Germany. He is the head of the System Security Lab at the Center for Advanced Security Research Darmstadt (CASED) and Scientific Director of Fraunhofer Institute for Secure Information Technology (SIT). Since January 2012 he has been the Director of the Intel Collaborative Research Institute for Secure Computing (ICRI-SC) at TU-Darmstadt. He holds a Ph.D. in computer science from the University of Saarland in Saarbrücken, Germany. Prior to academia, he worked in Research and Development of Telecommunications enterprises, such as Ericsson Telecommunications. He is on the Editorial Board of the *ACM Transactions on Information and System Security*.

Printed in the United States
by Baker & Taylor Publisher Services